B2B Exchanges

The Killer Application in the
Business-to-Business
Internet Revolution

*Arthur B Sculley and W William A
Woods*

ISIpublications

ISBN: 962-7762-59-8

To Jill and A, Sarah, Zoe and Ella, with all our love

www.B2Bexchanges.com
www.isipublications.com

Contents

Contents continued:

www.B2Bexchanges.com
www.isipublications.com

Preface

Every once in a while, a meeting of minds occurs as several hitherto unrelated thought processes converge. For us, the catalyst was a casual discussion about our experiences with developing stock exchanges and our joint and varied experience of E-commerce companies in the New Economy. As we talked, we realized that between us we have several areas of expertise which — when combined — create a potentially powerful knowledge set for any company proposing to establish or develop a business-to-business Exchange on the Internet.

Our securities market experiences, working with a number of stock exchanges over the last 15 years, are particularly relevant. Just as early tremors warn of an impending earthquake, the upheaval in the securities markets that Internet-based, electronic trading systems are causing is a signal of the huge changes that are to come in every major industry. The fact that electronic systems are shaking the very foundations of centuries- old stock exchange institutions should be a warning to us that no industry or company, however established they may be, will be spared. Every business will be shaken by this Internet quake.

The more we analyzed these new business-to-business Exchanges, the more we realized that they are the "killer application" of the business-to-business revolution. These new Internet exchanges can learn a lot from the way that stock exchanges have been structured and operated over the last 300 years. And there are a lot of things that B2B Exchanges must learn from securities markets *not* to do – especially in the light of the economic dynamics of "increasing returns" which are shaping the New Economy.

We have tried to set out the core principles of success for these new exchanges so that they can seize this unique opportunity and develop rapidly. In a "winner takes most" economy it is critical to move quickly and we hope that, by adopting some of the Secrets of Success described in this book, entrepreneurs that are starting B2B Exchanges can achieve their dreams. It would give us enormous satisfaction if this book were to help, at least in some small way, to influence the rapidly evolving New Economy.

This book draws mainly on examples from the US, because that is where the New Economy is developing the fastest. However, the business transformation that we describe is occurring worldwide and will now start to accelerate in Europe and Asia as companies learn from US experiences and fight to catch up.

The book has been targeted at senior management in Industrial Age companies and entrepreneurs who want to build a B2B Exchange, as well as at potential investors in B2B Exchanges. We hope that it will also appeal to the wider public, especially those employed in Industrial Age companies, and help them in some way to shape their own destiny and that of their employers.

When we started writing this book, B2B was a hot subject that was moving up to red hot. As we go to press, the subject is white hot. In such a compressed time space it is inevitable that some of what we say is going out of date as we write it. For this reason we have launched a web site at www.B2Bexchanges.com, to complement and update the information in this book as frequently as possible. Other parts are necessarily forward-looking projections that may or may not happen as soon as next week!

Our hope is that our web site will become a central information source for everyone involved in this exciting new area, and particularly that it will be an important on-line networking opportunity for B2B Exchanges.

For their role in the preparation of this book we wish especially to thank the following people: Sydney Price for her tireless research and editorial assistance. Sarah Barham, at ISI Publications, for editing the text and for having the faith in our ideas to agree to publish the book. Rakesh Sood and Jamie Friedman at Goldman Sachs Investment Research for allowing us to use their research data and for helping us to come up with some realistic estimates of the size of the B2B Exchange market space over the next four years. Charles Finnie at Volpe Brown & Whelan, for bouncing ideas around and for providing many insightful comments. Robbie Vorhaus and Bonni Broderick at Vorhaus & Co for their excellent PR advice. And Lee Petty in Bermuda for the cover design. However, we the authors must take joint and several responsibility for any errors or omissions that remain.

Foreword

After his retirement from JP Morgan, my brother, Arthur, agreed to become non-executive Chairman of the Bermuda Stock Exchange which is where he and William Woods — with his extensive stock exchange experience — first started to work together on what has become a successful undertaking; to transform a sleepy, local island stock exchange into an Internet-enabled, global stock exchange.

I wish I could say that I had fully appreciated five years ago how important Internet business-to-business (B2B) Exchanges would become. Yet looking at things today, it is obvious that business-to-business, and especially Internet, Exchanges where all kinds of commodities, financial instruments, intellectual properties, and various other goods and services can be electronically traded will be one of the most important pillars of the New Economy.

What probably most distinguishes the New Economy from the past is the shift in power from producers to customers, who now are in control of everything. Customers can demand — and expect to receive — the best quality, the best service and the lowest prices; they also want everything customized and they want it immediately. The Internet is enabling commerce to truly work on a global scale. Entrepreneurs can fundamentally re-invent how work gets done and give customers whatever they demand. It is no longer a competition between big and small, but between fast and slow. Innovation is highly rewarded, while traditional business size and stature is more often baggage than an advantage. Not since the invention of movable type over 500 years ago has the world experienced such a revolutionary change, but with one big difference; this time the change is many times larger and is happening many times faster than anything the world has ever experienced. Business-to-consumer companies certainly have grabbed the world's attention during the 1990s; however, many highly credible industry analysts have forecasted that the impact of business-to-business Internet companies will be many times larger than that of business-to-consumer.

The first wave of web companies were based on unique enabling technologies such as browsers, search engines, auctions, e-mail, chat, and various portal services. Building highly recognizable Internet brands set the pace so it's not surprising that these first generation Internet companies were started by high-technology entrepreneurs and backed by well-respected high-technology venture capitalists. But as the Internet moves toward B2B, it is now clear that traditional, large companies have no choice but to get into the game. Over the coming decade, we will see most corporations rush to re-invent themselves. We will see great global service economy centers like New York, Chicago, London, and Frankfurt jockey for position to lead various sectors of the Internet B2B industries. Small nations and regions, such as Hong Kong, Singapore, Israel, Ireland, Taiwan, Scandinavia, Australia, and Bermuda, with their advantage of speed, are also racing to become players in the New Economy. We will see B2B Exchanges becoming an important building block in the B2B global economy.

The best new companies will be those which take advantage of the Internet's unique strengths. Real-time, interactive communications and transactions which can be executed on a one-to-one basis are good examples. The Internet's power lies also in its ability to track and build histories as well as dynamically form co-operative buying groups, transact auctions, and provide instant and up-to-date information for informed deal making.

I have learnt a lot from my brother's experience in B2B Exchanges which we are now trying to adopt and apply in various derivative forms to some of our other Internet companies, both B2B and B2C. I think anyone who intends to build companies in the New Economy will find this book to be an extraordinarily useful and insightful guide.

John Sculley,
Partner,
Sculley Brothers LLC

Part I

Defining the B2B Market Space

Chapter 1:

What are B2B Exchanges?

If today's companies are to survive, they are going to have to reinvent themselves and integrate the Internet into everything they do.

The Jargon Jungle

The so-called Internet Revolution, or New Economy, has created many new companies, produced thousands of new millionaires and captured investors' attention to the point where it seems that every New York taxi driver is a day trader with some on-line brokerage service. But investors' attention has so far focused on companies that sell goods or services to the general public — what is now commonly called "business-to-consumer" transactions, or "B2C" for short — or that enable consumers to sell goods or services to each other — a "consumer-to-consumer" model, or "C2C". Another new economic model is "consumer-to-business", or "C2B", where the consumer states the price.

A good example of a B2C company is Amazon.com, Inc. (www.amazon.com), the on-line bookstore, or America Online, Inc. (www.aol.com), the Internet service and on-line content provider. A well-known example of a C2C company is eBay, Inc. (www.ebay.com), the popular on-line auctions company. eBay offers one big, "virtual" consumer trading community where individuals can buy and sell things from other individuals. An auction on eBay is, therefore, a good example of a C2C transaction on the Internet. An example of C2B is Priceline (www.priceline.com), where consumers indicate the price at which they are willing to buy a variety of goods and services, including airline tickets.

This book demystifies the jargon jungle and discusses the nature of business-to-business solutions on the Internet — that is "B2B" transactions. Some people, especially outside of the US, still regard the Internet as some sort of academic experiment or, at best, a low-security replacement for the telephone that allows individuals to send e-mails to each other. But over the last three years, especially in the US, the reliability and security issues associated with the early use of the Internet have been largely solved to the extent that every business is now adopting the Internet in one form or another. Now, some innovative new uses of the Internet by business are revolutionizing the way in which many goods and services are procured, priced, and distributed.

The quiet revolution that is developing in the world of B2B transactions will generate far more profits and millionaires than anything the C2C, B2C or C2B models can produce and will have a far more profound impact on the economy of each country than any number of Amazon.coms.

> B2B = Business-to-Business as in B2B Exchanges
> B2C = Business-to-Consumer as in Amazon.com
> C2C = Consumer-to-Consumer, as in users of eBay.com
> C2B = Consumer-to-Business, as in Priceline

The Power of the Network

Underlying this alphabet soup is a collection of silicon chips, copper wire and glass fibre — that is generically called the "Network". The Network connects all of the Internet-connected computers (over 200 million worldwide), as well as an increasing range of everyday devices that have silicon chips built into them (presently over two billion worldwide). The Network is currently being operated in accordance with the suite of communications standards called the Transmission Control Protocol/Internet Protocol — or TCP/IP.

Bob Metcalfe, the inventor of another networking standard called Ethernet, was the first person to notice that the value of a network increases by the square of the number of people or things connected to the network.

In other words, as the number of connections on a network increases in a linear fashion, the value of that network to its members increases on a compounding, or exponential, basis. If you owned a fax machine at a time when only two such machines existed, its value to you was modest. If you own a fax machine today, when there are more than 200 million such machines connected to the phone network, the ability to send and receive from each of those 200 million machines (a total of $200m-1^2$ possible connections) makes your machine exponentially more valuable to you. Incidentally, the Internet is so fundamentally changing the way that companies communicate with each other that you may shortly decide to consign your fax machine to the same cupboard where that old telex machine is stored.

Kevin Kelly, in his insightful book *New Rules for the New Economy* points out that the value of a network like the Internet actually increases faster than Bob Metcalfe's formula of n^2 (where n is the number of people connected). Metcalfe's network law is based on a telephone or fax network, where connections are point-to-point between two people. On the Network, we can make multiple simultaneous connections between groups of people so that the potential value of the network is not just $n \times n$, but n^n. We call this "Kelly's new law of networks".

The most dynamic example of this type of network is an on-line exchange, where multiple buyers and multiple sellers can come together in a virtual trading space.

The Internet Changes Everything

Once a company starts to integrate the Internet into what it does, it changes everything. Change starts with the way in which employees communicate with one another. Next to change is the way that the company sells and distributes its products, and then the way that the company communicates with other companies. For example, the way it communicates with its suppliers, the way it procures the goods and services it needs and the way in which it manages its whole supply chain. Finally, the Internet enables companies to move away from fixed pricing to dynamic pricing models (e.g, through the use of B2B Exchanges). This allows buying companies to significantly lower their acquisition costs, reduce inventory levels and ensure more on-time delivery of their products.

In this new environment, buying companies are becoming far more demanding as the Internet is creating a once-in-a-lifetime shift of power from the seller to the buyer.

B2B Markets are Enormous

Goldman Sachs Investment Research has analyzed the B2B marketplace and estimates that the value of transactions conducted on-line between companies will reach $1.5 trillion in the US by 2004.

Working with Goldman Sachs, we have estimated how much of this B2B Internet commerce will pass through B2B Exchanges in the US. We predict that on-exchange transactions will exceed $600 billion in value by 2004 in the US alone.

If B2B Exchanges can capture revenues representing just 0.5% of this turnover, they will collectively generate $3 billion in revenue per annum by 2004 — and that excludes the rest of the world.

By way of comparison, Forrester Research has estimated that total B2C on-line commerce in the US will reach just $108 billion by 2003.

B2B Exchanges

The power of the Network has resulted in the emergence of centralized marketplaces where businesses can buy and sell goods and services from each other. Just as centralized markets for the trading of stocks and bonds have become known as stock exchanges, we have given these exciting new business-to-business markets the name **B2B Exchanges**. Within the overall B2B revolution the unique features of these on-line exchanges have not yet caught the attention of the mainstream media or the average investor (our New York taxi driver, for instance). This book analyzes the profound nature of the changes that are occurring in B2B transactions as a result of the development of these Internet-based B2B Exchanges.

Based on their ability to bring buyers and sellers together on-line and thereby to create dynamic pricing, B2B Exchanges are the killer application in the business-to-business Internet revolution.

Defining a B2B Exchange

"Exchange: A building, office, institution, etc., used for the transaction of business or for monetary exchange." The New Shorter Oxford English Dictionary.

On the Internet every web site which enables buyers and sellers to come together and find each other is really a "virtual" exchange building. This book attempts to explain the phenomenon of formal B2B Exchanges as they are developing on the Web and describes the anatomy of a model B2B Exchange. We go on to analyze the key issues in building a successful, credible, and effective B2B Exchange.

In order to understand B2B Exchanges, we first have to define the term. Unlike the proverbial elephant, we may not be able to tell one when we see one! We will now attempt to set out a clear definition of a B2B Exchange and distinguish such an "exchange" from the tens of thousands of standard B2B E-commerce companies that already exist.

The unique feature of a B2B Exchange is that it brings multiple buyers and sellers together (in a "virtual" sense) in one central market space and enables them to buy and sell from each other at a dynamic price which is determined in accordance with the rules of the exchange.

The important point, which differentiates an exchange from other B2B E-commerce companies, is that an exchange involves **multiple** buyers and sellers and it centralizes and matches buy and sell orders and provides post-trade information. Contrast this with the procurement process of one company, say General Motors, which sets up a web site with an auction process for suppliers to bid on contracts with GM. This is NOT a B2B Exchange — although it is a B2B E-commerce site — because there is only one buyer. Similarly, a business that offers goods or services for sale to other businesses, over the Internet, is not an exchange, even if it provides a price-setting mechanism that is normally associated with an exchange, such as an auction — because there is only one seller.

Having multiple buyers and sellers creates its own special effects and necessitates a specialized approach to building a successful B2B Exchange versus a successful B2B E-commerce company. For example, as we explore in Chapters 5 and 11, an exchange must remain neutral and balance the competing interest of all its users — including buyers and sellers, shareholders and brokers and sometimes also take into consideration the public good.

Although we call these new, virtual market places "exchanges", they generally do not fall within the definition of a stock exchange or commodities exchange and they are not subject to registration with and regulation by government regulators — such as the US Securities and Exchange Commission (SEC) — which supervise securities markets and stock exchanges. B2B Exchanges are facilitating trades in goods and services such as paper, chemicals and insurance.

Four years ago there were no B2B Exchanges outside of the securities markets. Today there are around 100 such exchanges operating on the Internet.

Prominent examples of B2B Exchanges that we will use throughout this book are Catex, Chemdex, CreditTrade, e-STEEL, FreeMarkets, MetalSite, PaperExchange, PlasticsNet, and TechEx.

We have been involved as founders, investors, business partners or advisors in and to some of these exchanges. This book represents our current knowledge and experience of B2B Exchanges, and our experience in developing the Bermuda Stock Exchange (the BSX) as a fully-electronic exchange for the trading of securities.

The Winner Takes Most

Dr. James Martin, the author of *Cybercorp: The New Business Revolution*, is about to publish a new book called *Alien Intelligence: Winner Takes Most*, which demonstrates that the largest player, or "winner", in a particular vertical space will come to dominate that vertical because success is self-reinforcing in the New Economy. This powerful new paradigm derives from the fact that on the Network, success is driven by the dynamics of increasing returns rather than by the old laws of diminishing returns which plague Industrial Age companies.

As with securities markets, the more competing buyers and sellers that can be brought together in one place, the more liquid a market becomes and the more efficient the price-setting mechanism is. This creates a self-reinforcing mechanism whereby the sellers are attracted to the market with the most potential buyers and the increase in sellers makes that market space more attractive to more buyers, and so on — resulting in more transactions in that market.

Liquidity is king in the land of B2B Exchanges and, in accordance with the law of increasing returns, the most liquid exchange will be the winner.

The ubiquity and ease of use of the Internet means that people no longer have to be brought onto one physical trading floor to create liquidity. Increasingly inexpensive computing power and telecommunications are the weapons that allow Internet-based trading networks to challenge traditional trading mechanisms.

B2B Exchanges create an electronic, "virtual" marketplace that we call a market "space". Increasing returns will lead to a concentration of buyers and sellers in one B2B Exchange market space for each product.

One B2B Exchange may operate several market spaces, but only one market space is likely to dominate for each product.

Are ECNs B2B Exchanges?

One form of electronic trading that has attracted a high level of publicity in the traditional media to date is the Electronic Communications Network, or "ECN". ECNs are alternative securities trading systems that are generally privately owned and offer fully-automated, order routing and trade execution services. In effect, they are mini stock exchanges, but they don't like to call themselves that, and they don't offer all the services of a traditional stock exchange, because the SEC has not registered them as stock exchanges in the US. ECNs such as Archipelago, Instinet and Island offer a central market space where buy and sell orders are automatically matched — any order which does not match in the ECN is automatically routed onto another ECN or to a traditional stock exchange for execution. In our analysis, ECNs are definitely a form of exchange, but they are not solely B2B Exchanges. In the US, ECNs provide many institutional investors with anonymous trading opportunities, but they are also aimed at providing retail investors with low-cost execution-only services, in addition to extended trading hours and links to multiple exchanges. Therefore, using our definition, ECNs are a hybrid between a B2C and a B2B exchange.

ECNs have grown rapidly and there are now more than 50 alternative trading systems in the US, of which nine are registered as ECNs — including Archipelago, Instinet, Island and Strike, to name just a few leading systems. Recent SEC reports indicate that ECNs now trade more than 25% of Nasdaq's volume and 5% of the NYSE's.

ECNs have captured a greater share of Nasdaq's volume because they offer a more efficient price discovery function than the market-makers on Nasdaq. ECNs directly match buyers and sellers at the price that each is offering rather than at the bid-offer spread of the Nasdaq market-maker (who keeps the difference in the spread). The NYSE uses specialists to match buyers' and sellers' orders but, because it has greater liquidity, only about 10% of trades are made with the specialist. The remaining 90% of trades are matched directly at the buyer's and seller's offered price, which means that it is more efficient at setting the market price and, so far, it has lost less market share to ECNs.

In this book we use several lessons learnt from the success of ECNs to illustrate the Seven Secrets of Success for other B2B Exchanges, but we do not analyze any specific ECNs in great depth; they are a special phenomenon of securities markets and warrant their own dedicated study. However, as stock exchanges are one of the oldest forms of formalized exchange market, the rapid success of ECNs and their dynamic effects on more traditional stock exchanges are extremely important indicators of the potential for B2B Exchanges.

More Efficient Price Discovery

In the industrial economy, most prices are fixed by the seller, who publishes a catalog with non-negotiable prices. An alternative method to determine the price is to bring all the potential buy and sell orders together and let their competing offers set the highest price or the price which maximizes the amount sold. This is the approach adopted by ECNs with their central market-matching systems for securities. It is also the price discovery mechanism adopted by eBay to run its on-line auctions for consumers.

Increasingly, dynamic price-setting mechanisms are being used by many B2B Exchanges for business-to-business transactions, because the Internet's ability to interconnect companies very cheaply means that an Internet exchange can bring together bids and offers from all over the world.

In the New Economy, there has been a significant shift in economic power from the seller to the buyer. This is as true for B2B transactions as it is for B2C, C2C and C2B. On the Internet this truism is evident in the rapid rise of "reverse" or buyer-driven auctions. As we explore in Chapter 6, these auctions enable the buyer — for example, a company seeking to procure supplies — to solicit bids from multiple suppliers and watch the competition between those suppliers driving the procurement price *downwards* as the close of the auction approaches (hence the name "reverse auction"). B2B Exchanges are adopting reverse auctions to attract key buyers with the lure of substantial cost reductions for those big players.

Regulating the Market

Providing an open and fair market with complete transparency is a key element of an exchange's value proposition and enhances the exchange's ability to attract business. The exchange can only ensure that it is open and fair if it is prepared to regulate the users of the exchange's centralized market facility. The form of regulation most appropriate for Internet-based exchanges is what we call "self-regulation", whereby the B2B Exchange should be a self-regulatory organization, or SRO.

In Chapter 12, we explain why a successful B2B Exchange must regulate its own members in order to build credibility and integrity and to avoid calls for outside regulation.

Why B2B is Less Visible than B2C

Amazon.com, eBay and Yahoo! are already household names around the world. Companies like Catex, CreditTrade, Chemdex, e-STEEL, Elinex, MetalSite, PaperExchange and TechEx are relatively unknown to the general public, but are relatively well known in their chosen industry. Why is this? One obvious reason is that B2C companies market and sell to consumers — so we all hear about what they do. B2B Exchanges deal only with other businesses in their specific vertical industry sector, so they are naturally less visible to consumers and the media. Also, most of the so-called "dot com" IPOs have so far been by companies with B2C, C2C or C2B economic models.

Another factor is that many B2C companies are based on the West Coast of the US, which automatically attracts technology media attention because of Silicon Valley. The B2B Exchanges are more prominent on the East Coast and have not yet received widespread media attention.

This is beginning to change. An increasing number of media articles refer to the B2B revolution and an increasing number of securities analysts are focusing on B2B E-commerce. The recent successful IPO by the Internet Capital Group, Inc. has brought B2B E-commerce to the attention of Wall Street where the fastest future growth is now expected to be in B2B. The popular magazine, *Business 2.0* of the New Economy (www.business2.com) ran a series of articles in their September 1999 edition under the title "B2B Boom: The Web's Trillion Dollar Secret". Those investors, particularly institutional investors, who missed out on the B2C "dot com" phenomenon, are not going to be left out this time. If you are following the Internet commerce revolution, we believe that "you ain't seen nothing yet".

• • • • • • • • • • • • •

Chapter Summary:

- *B2B means Business-to-Business, B2C = Amazon, C2C = eBay, and C2B = Priceline.*
- *B2B E-commerce means potentially larger profits and cost savings than B2C markets.*
- *Bob Metcalfe's Law of Networks identified compounding growth in networks. Kevin Kelly's "new law of networks" identifies the additional exponential growth in the value of Internet networks.*
- *The Internet changes everything for companies.*
- *B2B markets are enormous compared to B2C transactions. Goldman Sachs Investment Research has estimated that the value of on-line B2B transactions in the US alone will reach $1.5 trillion by 2004.*
- *The authors predict that the value of B2B transactions passing through B2B Exchanges will exceed $600 billion by 2004. If B2B Exchanges can capture revenues representing just 0.5% of this turnover, they will collectively generate $3 billion in revenue per annum by 2004 — and that excludes the rest of the world.*
- *Based on the ubiquitous Internet technology, a large number of new companies are now establishing themselves as formal B2B Exchanges on the Web.*
- *Defining B2B Exchanges: The unique feature of a B2B Exchange is that it brings multiple buyers and sellers together (in a "virtual" sense) in one central market space and enables them to buy and sell from each other at a dynamic price which is determined in accordance with the rules of the exchange.*
- *Electronic Communications Networks (ECNs) are exchanges, but not strictly B2B Exchanges.*
- *B2B Exchanges must be differentiated from B2B E-commerce companies that offer products for sale, or seek to procure products, on-line, but represent only one buyer or one seller so that they do not bring multiple buyers and sellers together.*
- *Increasing returns mean that the winner will take most in each vertical space.*
- *There has been a lack of media hype about B2B compared to B2C and C2C, but this is changing.*

Authors' Note: Chapter 2 explores the way in which on-line B2B transactions in general are revolutionizing work flow patterns and will generate cost savings and increased profits on the Internet. We estimate the size of the B2B market space and describe the changes that the Internet is bringing about in corporations. Skip this chapter and go straight to Chapter 3 if you know about B2B generally and you want to get right into the details of B2B Exchanges.

Chapter 2:

B2B is Where the Profits Will Be, On-line

In Chapter 1 we looked at the acronyms that have been created to describe certain features of the New Economy. In this chapter, we attempt to establish the size of the B2B market space and describe how the Internet is revolutionizing business-to-business transactions.

Businesses are increasingly adopting Internet solutions because:

- interactive networks are now ubiquitous and inexpensive;
- they are becoming increasingly familiar with Internet technologies;
- there are low barriers of entry for companies to adopt Internet-based strategies;
- industry-wide standards such as extensible markup language (XML) are emerging that are cheaper, faster and better than the old Electronic Data Interchange (EDI) standards;
- the Internet is the ultimate global distribution system;
- they are hearing about, or actually experiencing, incredible cost savings and new revenue opportunities on-line; and
- the Internet offers the opportunity to revolutionize their supply chain management.

As more companies adopt Internet-based B2B applications, other companies will have to follow them just to stay competitive. This revolution is just beginning, and explosive growth is inevitable.

Size of the B2B Market Space

The two main industry consultants who provide reliable estimates of the size of E-commerce generally are International Data Corp. (IDC) and Forrester Research Inc. IDC states that they expect B2B on-line commerce to "explode as the Web becomes an accepted vehicle for volume B2B purchases". In IDC's Internet Commerce Market Model (Version 5.1), they estimate that B2B on-line commerce in the US alone will rise from $50 billion in 1999 to $633 billion in 2003. Forrester Research shows that inter-company trade of hard goods over the Internet in the US hit $43 billion in 1998 and they estimate that it will be $109 billion in 1999 and will reach $1.3 trillion by 2003, an annual growth of 99%. This number already excludes any "soft" goods or services sold over the Internet between businesses, which Forrester estimates will be worth $200 billion by 2003. By comparison, Forrester says that the total B2C on-line commerce market was worth just $8 billion in 1998 and estimates that B2C spending on-line will be just $108 billion in 2003.

The difference in the two estimates for B2B on-line commerce may be due to the differing definitions of E-commerce and methodologies used by each company. However, Goldman Sachs' equity analysts in their research department have reviewed the numbers and come up with their own proprietary estimates for B2B Internet commerce. Goldman Sachs Investment Research endorses the higher figure as they estimate that the B2B on-line commerce market in the US alone will reach $1.5 trillion by 2004.

What is already clear then, is that B2B Internet commerce will be enormous and will be approximately ten times the size of B2C on-line commerce.

Not only is the B2B E-commerce market already much larger than that for B2C, but it is predicted to grow much more rapidly.

The Technology of Communicating is Now Invisible

Previous efforts to "wire" companies together were based on EDI standards. EDI is a closed technology that costs companies hundreds of thousands of dollars to implement. Each business in the network has to be linked in by dedicated connections. Every industry that seeks to implement EDI in order to facilitate E-commerce has to start off by defining the standards that will allow one company's invoicing system to talk to another company's back-office ordering system and then it has to build the physical connections, or dedicated network, and license the software to link those computer systems together. Every time a new supplier or customer is added to the system, the procedure has to be repeated.

Over the last four years, the reliability, speed, and security of the Internet have improved to the point where more businesses are connecting to the Internet and traditional businesses are now using the Internet to conduct E-commerce and to exchange information with customers, suppliers, and distributors. With the widespread adoption of Internet technologies by businesses over the last four years and the acceptance of standards like extensible markup language (XML) as the best way to exchange information on-line, there is now one ubiquitous EDI mechanism which, remarkably, requires no more than a web browser on a PC with Internet access to get connected.

Successful manufacturers are now quickly moving away from company-unique IT systems to open, data-rich and flexible links with supply partners built around an Internet core.

All enterprise resource planning systems are now designed to be fully EDI compliant and XML capable, which also allows manufacturers committed to expensive EDI networks to connect with those suppliers who find EDI cost-prohibitive.

The issues are no longer, how do we communicate? How do we build a physical connection between us? Rather, what are we going to use this amazing new form of connectivity to do? What are the business applications that we should develop on this network?

The technology of how businesses communicate and what network businesses use is now as invisible as the wonders of electricity when we switch on the porch light.

Use of the Internet for Sales and Marketing

When businesses first start using the Internet they tend to use it to do the same things they have done before — but cheaper, faster, and often better. Initially, the Internet has the greatest impact on businesses in the areas of sales and marketing and corporate communications — through the launch of a corporate web site and the adoption of e-mail.

For instance, companies take their existing brochure or catalog and put up an attractive web site, which is often referred to as "brochureware". Then they notice that they can update the web site more regularly than they used to print their catalog and that the cost of updating the web site is minimal. Then they notice that they can adjust the prices of the items listed on the web site more easily than they can change their printed catalog. Then they start to get feedback directly from customers who have visited the web site and send e-mail comments. This may be a revelation to those firms that have always sold to wholesalers or retail stores and have never really dealt with individual customers before.

In the area of corporate communications the power of e-mail is instantly effective in spreading information within the organization and empowering the knowledge workers — enabling them to spend more time on strategic thinking about the company's market space, products, processes, and profitability.

As Bill Gates states in his book *Business @ The Speed of Thought: Using a Digital Nervous System,* successful companies need to have some kind of nervous system. In the New Economy, that nervous system must be a digital nervous system that ensures that information flows through the organization by e-mail, by shared databases and through collaborative applications. An immediate effect of introducing the Internet into a company is that valuable information is shared much more easily among — and is obtained much more quickly by — the people in the company who need it.

How the Internet can create distribution channel conflicts

Take an imaginary company which has posted its products on the Internet. One day a bright member of staff points out that the company could sell its products directly off the web site and ship them direct to the end consumer. Senior management struggles with this for a while because they realize that it will upset their current distribution channels, through which they have been doing business for many years. Finally they take the plunge and start to sell directly off their web site, by commerce-enabling the site. The company is now conducting Internet commerce. The process we describe here has already occurred in thousands of small businesses and hundreds of large businesses worldwide, including companies the size of Compaq Computer and General Motors, for example.

The Internet, a simple communications tool that started out letting them put their corporate brochure and product catalog on-line has suddenly revolutionized the company's sales and distribution system. What started out as a traditional B2B company has been transformed into a B2C company, simply by putting its products on-line.

How B2B Can Become B2C

Pre-Internet

Factory ➤➤➤➤➤ Distribution channels➤➤➤➤➤ Customer
(manage inventory)

Post Internet

Factory ➤➤➤➤➤ Company web site ➤➤➤➤➤ Customer
(direct sales)

This transformation is not without its shocks. The first shock is to the firm's existing distribution channels. Now that the firm is selling to customers directly there is a potential conflict with its previous distribution channels. For instance, if the firm has a whole range of franchised store-owners, those stores are going to lose sales to the web site. This potential conflict can be so enormous that it prevents the company embracing the Internet. For example, Toys "R" Us has recently announced that it has abandoned a proposed joint venture with Benchmark Partners that was intended to fund and launch a new on-line business operation. Apparently the venture failed because Toy "R" Us was not prepared to let the on-line business compete directly with its retail stores because the channel conflicts would upset the store managers of their existing retail stores worldwide. Similarly, Amway Corporation, the direct–selling business could potentially end up competing with all of its three million individual business owners (IBOs), who act as distributors, now that it has launched an on-line business at www.Quixtar.com. However, Amway has adopted an innovative approach to avoid conflicts between its new direct sales web site and its worldwide network of IBOs, by prompting customers to enter the identification number of the IBO who referred them when making each on-line purchase. In this way the IBOs can still earn payments from the direct, on-line sales channel.

The next shock for our simple case study with a fictitious company comes quickly. One day it receives an order from overseas. An Internet user in Japan has visited its web site and ordered direct from them. They suddenly realize that overnight they have become a global company. The company's web site is available from anywhere in the world and is open for business 24 hours a day, seven days a week, 365 days per year — unlike any bricks and mortar retail store. This leads to a complete rewrite of the firm's marketing strategy and customer focus. Instead of focusing exclusively on how to make its products, the company now has to focus on how those products reach the customer and how to keep those customers happy. In other words, the manufacturer of the product is now responsible for the customer care aspects as well.

How the Internet is Re-inventing Work Flow

The above example is rather simplistic, but it describes the basic process that thousands of companies around the world have been going through in the last five years as a result of introducing the Internet into their business.

More recently, use of the Internet has been working a rather more sophisticated magic on business-to-business relationships. Many companies now consider the Internet crucial for the procurement of goods from suppliers, the management of their supply chain, and product development.

Underlying this change is the basic fundamental, that the Internet is all about creating low-cost, universal communications between people, between companies, between computers run by companies and between the assets owned by companies, with instantaneous delivery of critical information, such as the receipt of a new order, to each and every party that needs that information.

In addition to computers, anything that contains a silicon chip is capable of being connected to the Network and of sending and receiving information. That information may be as simple as stating whether that particular item is on or off, empty or full, hot or cold; or it may be more sophisticated information such as where it is currently located (as determined by satellite-based GPS) and what it is doing. Whatever the information, its value to the organization can be enormous and it can totally re-invent the company's work flow.

For companies that make products, the Internet now offers the opportunity to tie together all of the suppliers and shippers that the company deals with. The manufacturer, the suppliers, and the shippers can then track the manufacturing process from raw material delivery through to delivery of the product to the customer. Inventory levels, production schedules, and delivery dates are all available to everyone that needs to know.

Once a company integrates the Internet into everything it does at this level, it can completely re-engineer its supply chain management and re-invent the firm's whole business model.

Enabling the build-to-order model

Take the supply chain management of large manufacturers like General Motors and Ford Motor Co. Car manufacturers deal with thousands of suppliers in order to procure all of the parts (including some highly intelligent silicon chips) that now make up the average production-model motor car. In the past, companies like GM and Ford sought to manage all of those relationships through an extremely expensive EDI-based system that tried to tie together the multiplicity of different computer systems that each of these suppliers use. The EDI system was intended to enable the procurement orders issued by the manufacturer to be automatically accepted by the internal systems of the suppliers and for the suppliers' invoices to be automatically recognized, authenticated and validated by the manufacturer's mainframe computers. A substantial part of the cost of building that system was the cost of setting up a physical network that allowed all of these remote firms to communicate with the manufacturer and in licensing the software for each supplier.

Companies like GM and Ford are now moving all of this communication between suppliers onto the Internet. Instead of running a huge network and struggling to get systems to talk to each other, the manufacturer is now able to add new suppliers at any time and to have a two-way dialog with the suppliers — which represents a completely new way to manage supply chains.

Part of this new methodology is enabling those suppliers to post their catalog on-line for the manufacturer's procurement managers and for the manufacturer to run reverse auctions in which a short list of pre-qualified suppliers are asked to bid on a large procurement contract with the manufacturer. As we shall see in Chapter 6, the reverse auction process can significantly reduce a company's purchase costs by making suppliers compete on price. Companies like GM and Ford claim that these new trading mechanisms have reduced their procurement costs by a staggering 25% on some items.

In Chapter 3, we explore the way in which third-party B2B Exchanges are extending the role of the Internet in creating dynamic pricing models and dramatic costs savings for companies.

In a *Wall Street Journal* article of 11 August 1999, by Fara Warner, the reporter disclosed that this new Network with GM's suppliers and the enhanced web site maintained by GM at www.gm.com has enabled GM to entertain the concept of building cars to order. Of course, computer manufacturers have been doing this for several years. Michael Dell of Dell Computers has perfected the direct sales technique and now sells more than $12 million worth of computers from the www.dell.com web site each day (seven days a week) but only builds each of those computers after the order has been received.

Now imagine if you could research your next automobile purchase on-line. You select the various features you want from the selections on the web site and then order it immediately, with your exact specification and color preference, and maybe even apply for a loan on-line. Behind the scenes, GM will not even start building that vehicle until your order and payment (or loan) has been cleared. **Less than one week later, your tailor-made car will be delivered to your door.**

GM's web site enables the company to communicate directly with the customer in this way. By sharing information electronically with its suppliers, GM knows when to expect the parts needed to assemble a particular car, and can schedule assembly accordingly. Suppliers can tap into GM's order systems to find out what the company needs even before the parts order comes through, so they have the part ready to ship as soon as the order is placed. This creates enormous cost savings for the manufacturer by reducing the amount of parts inventory it has to hold and it also helps ensure more "on time" product deliveries.

Unfortunately, the same *Wall Street Journal* article suggests that this is still all a pipe dream for GM. Not because GM lacks the technology or know-how to do this, but rather because the autoworkers union in the US has so far prevented GM from using supplier-provided pre-built modules, which are critical in a "build-to-order" production line.

Globalization

According to a recent study released by Andersen Consulting (www.ac.com), until now, most revenues and therefore the greatest economic impact of E-commerce has been in the US where the E-commerce and IT industries together account for a third of real economic growth over the past three years. But Europe is rapidly eroding the US's lead. Andersen predicts that by 2002, European E-commerce revenues are expected to equal 55% of the US total. By 2003, the on-line population of the European Union is expected to match that of the US. In a similar survey released in 1998, Andersen found that most European companies used the Internet almost exclusively for sales and marketing.

In 1999, however, more than a third of the European executives surveyed by Andersen had expanded their plans, saying that they now consider the Internet crucial for the procurement of goods and services from suppliers, logistics, finance, and product development.

Within five years, no fewer than 90% expect to use E-commerce in sales and marketing and 83% in procurement. However, most European executives acknowledged that, to date, their commitment to E-commerce has lagged behind that of their US counterparts.

All around the world, corporate spending on integrating the Internet into everything a company does is bound to accelerate after the need to spend the IT budget on Y2K fixes is over.

Intermediaries and Infomediaries

Intermediaries who act as brokers between buyers and sellers service many business-to-business markets. In markets which lack price transparency and where it is difficult to find out who is buying or selling at any one point in time, the broker's role is to facilitate the ability of buyers to find sellers at the right time and at a mutually acceptable price. The Chinese have a proverb that (loosely translated) states: "Big fish only grow in murky water". Applied to B2B markets, a lack of transparency in a market sometimes allows brokers to dominate the market and dictate large commission payments based on the value of the transaction, rather than the value of the services actually provided by them. In such markets, the brokers restrict the free flow of information. For example, they ensure that the prices at which trades are made are not widely disseminated and that the knowledge of who is buying and selling in the market is tightly controlled.

In the securities markets, the traditional stockbrokers have controlled access to timely information about stocks. Pre-Internet, unless you were able to afford to buy a terminal from an information vendor for several hundred dollars a month, the only way that you could access timely stock quotes and research was through a broker. This enabled the stockbrokers to charge high commissions. Today, the Internet has enabled on-line brokers to offer stock quotes and access to research data for a fixed commission per trade at rates as low as $8 for trades that would cost over a $100 through a full-service traditional broker. Another good example of such a market is the reinsurance market, which is dominated by a few large brokers who control the flow of information between primary insurers and the underwriters at the reinsurance companies. In some reinsurance deals, commissions as high as 10% of the amount of the premium are paid to the broker who arranges the deal. Similarly, in the plastics business middlemen reportedly charge 30-50% commission on some products.

In such markets, a successful B2B exchange can have the same effect as a burst of strong sunlight on a murky pond. As the sunlight burns off the algae the water clears — buyers and sellers can then identify themselves more easily, price quotes and the prices of concluded transactions start to circulate, and the market starts to become more transparent. Some brokers may therefore resist the introduction of a B2B Exchange in such market spaces, although many are now recognizing the inevitability of this process and are focusing on providing more value-added services to their customers.

B2B Exchanges will not necessarily destroy the role of intermediaries, but they will often completely redefine that role.

In fact, it is more common for the exchange to merely change the role of the broker and require them to demonstrate the value they add and only to charge commissions (often on a fixed-fee basis) that better reflect the value that they add. For example, in the reinsurance world, the introduction of a B2B Exchange like Catex has not precipitated the demise of the insurance brokers. Many insurers still feel more comfortable using a broker as an intermediary to handle the deal-making process — **but there is a marked trend towards lower commissions and fixed fees for consultancy services**.

In their new book *Net Worth*, John Hagel III (co-author of *Net Gain*) and Marc Singer of McKinsey & Company, Inc. focus on the potential for building new business models on the Internet, rather than just doing the same things faster and cheaper. *Net Worth* postulates that, whilst there will be some disintermediation through use of the Internet, there will also be entirely new classes of intermediary enabled by the Internet. In fact the authors state that they believe that the most significant opportunities for value creation on the Internet will consist of building new kinds of intermediaries that help to shift value from vendors to customers. They call such a firm an information intermediary or "infomediary". Although their book is primarily focused on the potential for infomediaries to develop between business vendors and consumers (i.e. in the B2C and C2B space), Hagel and Singer's ideas can be applied to B2B markets.

In B2B markets, the B2B Exchanges themselves act as a form of new infomediary since they often empower and advance the interests of the buyer.

For example, one form of B2B Exchange that is developing is an infomediary who represents business buyers and aggregates their information with that of other buyers and uses the combined market power to negotiate with, and seek, competitive bids from suppliers on their behalf. Shop2gether (www.shop2gether.com) is just such a B2B Exchange with a specific focus on aggregating the purchase orders of small businesses.

Profits on the Internet?

So far, successful B2C Internet companies have not been associated with the word "profit". Amazon.com, for example now has a market capitalization in excess of $23 billion and claims that it stocks over 4.7 million titles — but it has not made a quarterly profit since it started in business. In fact, Amazon.com had accumulated losses to end 1998 of more than $150 million. The people who have made profits from the rapid growth of Amazon are the courier companies who distribute the books, the professional advisors who took them public and the investors who bought early and have already sold.

eBay is an exception to the rule — it had net income of $800,000 in its latest quarter. But this small profit was generated on revenue of $49.5 million in that period and supports a market valuation of $28 billion.

However, analysts argue that in the New Economy an Internet company should be valued based on its gross revenue not net income, and that those few B2C companies which come to dominate the Web will make monster profits in the future.

The point here is that young Internet companies are often valued by their next year's forecast revenues which demonstrate the success of their business model, market share, ability to scale up quickly, and leadership position. That basis of valuation may or may not be valid in B2C, but what is clear is that B2B E-commerce has the potential to generate substantially larger profits than B2C commerce.

Consider the economics of a book sale like this one with a ticket price of, say, $30. A common division of the spoils is as follows: author 10%, publisher 10%, wholesale distributor 50%, retail store or Amazon.com 30%. Note that within this chain the main revenue is generated by the B2B transactions. The publishing business feeds the wholesale distributor, and takes 10% or more, and the wholesale business feeds the retail store or Amazon, and keeps 50% or more — over 60% ($18) of the value is generated in the B2B transactions.

It follows that, if Internet-based efficiencies can reduce the costs of the businesses involved in the middle of the production and supply chain, then the resulting increase in profits will be greater in the B2B portion of the process than in the B2C piece (that is, the sale by the retail store to the consumer).

Translate this theoretical example to the world of B2B procurements. Business-to-business markets where brokers use the telephone or the mail to sell products and generate commissions of 10% or more are now being targeted by B2B Internet-based exchanges. These B2B Exchanges can reduce transaction costs to less than 1% — and the difference will mainly represent increased profits for the businesses and revenue for the B2B Exchange.

Some of these B2B markets are enormous in value. For example, the market for paper in the US is worth at least $260 billion per year (PaperExchange), the market for steel sold in the US is $600 billion per year (MetalSite and e-STEEL), the market for plastics is $370 billion per year (PlasticsNet), and the market for re-insurance in the US is at least $100 billion per year in premiums alone. Compare this with the US market for books which is just $25 billion per year. In addition, the average sticker price on most of these B2B procurement contracts is not $30, but more like $30,000, so the potential for cost savings and higher profit margins in the middle are much higher than for low ticket consumer items like books and CDs.

• • • • • • • • • • • • • •

Chapter Summary:

- *Explosive growth in B2B markets is inevitable.*
- *Forrester Research Inc. shows that inter-company trade of hard goods over the Internet hit $43 billion last year and could reach $1.3 trillion by 2003, an annual growth rate of 99%. Goldman Sachs' research confirms that business-to-business Internet commerce in the US will reach $1.5 trillion by 2004.*
- *Companies initially use the Internet for sales and marketing — with "brochureware".*
- *An on-line business strategy can quickly turn a company into a B2C company and create channel conflicts with retail stores.*
- *Now companies are applying the Internet to procurement, logistics, finance, and even product development.*
- *Advanced use of the Internet to contact customers and simultaneously tie together suppliers in the production process will enable customers to order products on-line — such as a customized car — and then sit back, confident that the car will be built to their specification and delivered to their door within a few days.*
- *B2B Exchanges are challenging some market intermediaries to redefine their roles.*
- *B2B Exchanges are creating new opportunities as a form of "infomediary".*
- *Profits on the Internet? Since the business-to-business portion of many manufacturing processes includes the majority of the value of a product, the potential cost savings and increased profits in B2B transactions are much higher than in B2C.*

Chapter 3:

Why B2B Exchanges are Developing on the Internet

As we saw in Chapter 2, in many cases the use of the Internet by business has so far been largely confined to the sales and marketing area. The first attempts at E-commerce on-line mainly involved the transfer of traditional business models to the Internet.

Amazon.com is a classic example of this. Despite its enormous early mover advantage and tremendous image as an Internet innovator, its original business model still involved the traditional distribution channels for books. Produced by a publisher, sold through a wholesale distributor to a retailer (albeit one selling on the Internet only), and then on to the consumer through a centralized, physical warehouse (acting as a fulfilment center for the dispatch of the books). Another excellent example of early Internet success is Cisco Systems, the people who make the "plumbing" that operates the Network. Cisco sells all its routers, bridges etc. on-line in a classic transfer of the existing business model onto the Network. But new customers cannot buy from Cisco directly on-line — they must first set up an account with Cisco.

The innovation, to the extent that it existed early on, was in the use of the Internet to connect with existing partners to exchange information more easily (e-mail) or in moving the existing product catalog onto the Web for on-line sales. The price-setting mechanism for those products on-line, has initially remained the same — the supplier establishes a non-negotiable fixed price prior to the marketing of the product.

33

For example, although Amazon.com has subsequently moved into the C2C auction business, it quotes a fixed price for books and CDs and has not yet moved to let consumers bid on the retail price of its book catalog through on-line auctions. As we shall see, Amazon will probably do just that, at least in respect of older titles or to clear surplus stock, in the near future.

New B2B Business Models On-line

The scene is now evolving at high speed, with the Internet spawning truly innovative new business models in the B2B market space. Forrester Research has identified three **new** models, which are indigenous to the Internet: aggregators, auctions and exchanges. We would add two further categories: trading hubs and "post and browse". Each of these types of trading mechanism is analyzed in more detail in Chapter 6.

Unique Internet B2B models defined

Aggregators. A one-stop shopping venue for procurement by companies. The aggregator streamlines purchasing by aggregating the product catalogs of many suppliers in one place and in one format. Parts and products displayed on-line can number in the hundreds of thousands.

Examples: e-Chemicals, Chemdex, MetalSite, PlasticsNet

Trading Hubs. These sites build buyer and seller communities for multiple verticals that have not yet embraced the Internet themselves in a specific exchange. Sellers are given virtual storefronts to advertise their products and buyers are attracted by news, product specification information, product reviews and product recommendations. Trading hubs can be purely "horizontal" in that they try to support all the buyers and sellers in many different industries. Alternatively, they can be "diagonal" in that they specialize in supporting a specific type of buyer or seller, or a specific type of product category across multiple industries. Trading hubs may provide an auction sale mechanism for large items with infrequent sales or an auction procurement process for aggregated small buyers.

Examples: Horizontal: FreeMarkets, VerticalNet; Diagonal: Shop2gether, Tradeout

Post and Browse Markets. Essentially a sophisticated Bulletin Board where buyers and sellers can post expressions of interest to buy or sell. After "meeting" through the postings on the Board, the parties negotiate a deal between themselves. The Internet enables buyers and sellers from all around the world to participate on-line. This is the ideal mechanism for very fragmented markets with non-standardized products because each contract is quite different and requires one-on-one negotiation. These markets have the goal of moving the industry towards more standardized contracts which can then be traded in a more automated manner.

Examples: Catex, CreditTrade, Elinex, TechEx

Auction Markets. A revolutionary new pricing model for many markets in which multiple buyers or sellers bid competitively on a contract. This is the ideal mechanism for liquidating surplus at best possible prices as it enables a wide range of potential buyers to bid competitively for the products at below-market prices.

Examples: e-STEEL, Manheim Online, CattleOfferings

Fully-automated Exchanges. A centralized market for standardized (or commodity-like) products. Competitive bidding between multiple buyers and sellers, with automated matching of orders, creates an efficient price-setting mechanism on-line.

Examples: e-STEEL, PaperExchange (Catex, CreditTrade, and Elinex are moving towards this space).

Source: Forrester Research, Inc., and the Authors

In this book we focus on the development of the B2B Exchanges — which includes the trading hub, post and browse, auction and automated exchange models.

Common Features of B2B Exchanges

B2B Exchanges are very similar to other exchanges that provide a neutral, centralized market space, such as stock exchanges. In the same way that stock exchanges operate, B2B Exchanges provide the following key advantages:

- centralized market space;
- neutrality;
- standardized contracts, documents, and products;
- pre-qualification and regulation of the users;
- dissemination of price quotes, post-trade information and pricing history;
- maintenance of the integrity of the market;
- transparency;
- self-regulation of the market and of the pricing mechanism;
- clearing and settlement, or fulfilment services;
- confidentiality and anonymity; and
- an exchange community — a meeting place not only for members and users, but also for service providers.

In Part II of this book we analyze each of these features in detail.

Net Effect

The reasons why the Internet is enabling exchanges to develop where they have not existed previously include:

- on-line markets operate at a fraction of the physical-world costs;
- the low cost of getting connected, irrespective of geographical distance, enables fragmented buyers and sellers to find each other (i.e. global reach);
- new price-setting mechanisms, such as on-line auctions, can improve pricing efficiency and/or increase volumes traded;
- automated trading and anonymity can eliminate many market inefficiencies; and
- centralized markets generate trading and pricing information (i.e. transparency) that did not exist before.

Challenging an entrenched market with a new B2B Exchange is only possible if the new entrant can build liquidity at much lower cost. Increasingly cheap computing power and telecommunications bandwidth is what allows B2B Exchanges to challenge trading floors and other traditional trading networks.

Lower costs of operation

The industrial world has created trading relationships based on three communications channels: face-to-face contact, telephone calls and the mail. Face-to-face contacts evolved from the "coffee shop" style markets (e.g. Lloyd's insurance market in the nineteenth century) to open outcry trading in physical pits (e.g. The Chicago Board of Trade (CBOT) for derivatives trading). Telephone-based markets have been improved by the use of recording machines to record the trades, fax machines to send trade confirms and computer screens to display indicative prices or quotes. The physical mail has improved from the days of the pony express and the clipper ship travel times to 24-hour delivery for most domestic destinations and only a few days for international mail. In addition, courier companies now provide guaranteed delivery of documents almost anywhere in the world within a few days.

However, none of these methods of communication can compete with the almost instantaneous, low-cost delivery of information, to any computer anywhere in the world, which is the hallmark of the Internet — both for e-mail messages and web-based applications.

An on-line, electronic market does not require a trading floor — for which physical real estate is at a premium — in order to create a centralized market space.

Consider that the NYSE is planning to build a bigger trading floor of over 100,000 square feet in Manhattan to house the more than 6,000 floor brokers, specialists, computer technicians, and miscellaneous clerks it requires to keep the vast trading floor running smoothly. After the NYSE threatened to move to New Jersey, the Mayor of New York City agreed that taxpayers would pay the more than $600 million bill for this new floor. Since 1994, the NYSE has spent more than $1 billion in developing technologies that deliver orders into the physical floor more quickly. And the CBOT has just spent $182 million to build a huge new trading floor that can house up to 8,000 traders. Combined with the existing agricultural complex, the CBOT now boasts the world's largest contiguous trading hall at 92,000 square feet, a space large enough to house two Jumbo jets. Compare that with the ability of an ECN, like Archipelago Holdings, to launch an Internet-based "virtual" trading floor which is accessible from anywhere in the world, with a few small computers and for a very modest cost.

At the CBOT, physical real estate on that expensive trading floor is at a premium as each contract type (i.e. product) has to be traded in its own physical "pit" — a ring or trading post where the traders gather round. This means that any new contracts that do not succeed in achieving volume quickly are removed and replaced with other products and the cost of launching a new product is enormous. In 1997, the CBOT launched options and futures based on the Dow Jones Industrial Average for the first time and had to spend millions of dollars just to fit out the trading pit for the launch.

On an electronic system, the cost of adding another product to the on-line catalog or another contract to the list is almost zero. Similarly, the cost of maintaining a listing for a contract or product is very low, so that new products can be given time to develop a market.

Global reach and "one-stop shopping"

The cost of accessing the Internet is falling daily and the cost of sending information by e-mail or over the Web is a fraction of standard telephone, fax, and mail costs. This means that sellers can reach out to buyers all over the world and the buyers can access sellers all over the world. In the physical world, businesses and individual consumers will often pay a higher price or buy an inferior product simply because that is the only service available in their physical location. Now B2B Exchanges are able to bring fragmented buyers and sellers together on the "virtual" trading floor of the centralized market space.

B2B Exchanges create a community of those buyers and sellers in a structured and organized fashion. After viewing the offers posted on the exchange, communications between potential buyers and sellers are specifically targeted to the interested parties. The on-line exchange thus generates great sales leads to pre-qualified buyers. Unlike e-mail on the Internet generally, communications through a central exchange can be organized, encrypted, authenticated, time-stamped, tracked, and verified.

The low cost of getting connected, irrespective of geographical distance, enables fragmented buyers and sellers to find each other through a B2B Exchange without incurring real-world search and travel expenses or high commissions for using intermediaries. In addition, by aggregating multiple sellers in one place, an exchange creates a one-stop shopping experience for the buyers.

This will force traditional intermediaries, like brokers, to redefine their roles in B2B markets but will create new opportunities for "infomediaries".

More efficient price discovery

In the industrial economy, most prices are set by the seller, who generally has the greater economic power, and can publish a catalog with non-negotiable prices. An alternative method is to bring together all the potential buy and sell orders at any particular time and let those competing offers set the highest price or the price which maximizes the amount sold. Then that price can truly be called the market price at that particular point in time.

Dynamic pricing — through competitive bidding and auction systems — is one of the most exciting features of B2B Exchanges and, as we shall explore in Chapter 6, it represents a key component of the revolutionary nature of B2B Internet commerce.

Auction pricing is the approach adopted by ECNs with their central market matching systems for securities. It is also the price discovery mechanism adopted by eBay to run its on-line markets. Increasingly, it is the price-setting mechanism being used by many B2B Exchanges, as the Internet can bring together bids and offers from all over the world, with its ability to interconnect companies cheaply.

As with securities markets, the more competing buyers and sellers that can be brought together, the more liquid the market becomes and the more efficient the price-setting mechanism is.

For example, in the US securities industry, ECNs are creating more efficient order execution and pricing, than on the traditional stock exchanges like Nasdaq (Nasdaq stands for the National Association of Securities Dealers' Automated Quotations) and the NYSE. Nasdaq has been particularly affected by ECNs, starting with the success of Instinet (a Reuters company) and now multiplied by the launch of around 50 proprietary trading systems, of which around ten have been approved by the SEC as ECNs.

The reason for this is that Nasdaq operates a "quotation" system whereby market-makers make quotes to buy or sell a security and a consumer's order is executed against the market-makers prices. The market-maker ensures that there is a gap between the "bid" (the buy price) and the "ask" (the sell price) so that he makes a profit on each trade. This gap is known as the "spread" and represents a hidden cost of dealing on Nasdaq, because consumers' orders are not matched at the best price each is willing to pay, but rather at the prices set by the market-maker. This hidden cost is justified if there is low liquidity in a particular stock. Because the market maker is then adding value by ensuring that there is always a bid and ask price, even if there are not two consumers looking to buy and sell at that particular point in time.

Nasdaq was developed to trade small capitalization stocks which could not be listed on the NYSE and which were generally illiquid. As some of the companies on Nasdaq grew, such as Microsoft and Dell Computers, Nasdaq became much more liquid; the "blue chip" stocks naturally no longer required market-makers. However, the market-makers refused to allow Nasdaq to develop a central matching engine (called a "central limit order book") that would allow consumers' orders to be matched directly at a single price. In fact, an SEC investigation in the mid–1990s discovered that many market-makers were also colluding to fix the spreads in some stocks. Based on this discovery, the SEC introduced new order handling rules in January 1997 which require a market-maker to trade at the price specified by the customer if he has a buy and a sell order at the same price.

This has enabled ECNs to step into the market and offer central limit order books that match orders at the best price (i.e. the price at which the buyer and the seller have indicated that they are willing to trade). Any order that cannot be matched in the ECN's order book is routed to Nasdaq for execution against a market-maker. The problem for Nasdaq is that these ECNs are effectively sucking liquidity out of Nasdaq and leaving the market-makers with only those trades that cannot be filled quickly by the ECN. From the consumer's point of view, the ECNs have created a more efficient mechanism for matching orders and thus reduced their trading costs. This has enabled ECNs to attract more than 25% of Nasdaq's trading volume away from Nasdaq on a daily basis.

More transparency

Most markets operate with less than perfect information about prices of similar deals or about supply and demand. Once a centralized exchange develops, the pricing, volumes, and trading history become available to all users in a way that was not possible before.

The traditional world of B2B reinsurance is a good example. In the past, primary insurers obtained quotes for reinsurance from wholesale reinsurers through an insurance broker. The broker would cultivate relationships with several key reinsurers (or "markets") in order to obtain the best quotes for the primary insurer and the best commissions for the broker. In order to protect their markets the brokers do not share the pricing information amongst themselves or amongst their clients, so there is no transparency in the pricing process. Primary insurers do not know what other companies are paying for reinsurance and so, by controlling that information, the brokers have been able to charge commissions of up to 10% on multimillion-dollar premiums.

Now that Catex has established a B2B Exchange for insurance products, the price at which reinsurance contracts are executed through the system is immediately broadcast on the Internet to all registered users. But every trade report is fully anonymous, so that other users do not know who the parties to the contract are. Brokers are still used in the system, but now each broker is giving up the confidentiality regarding the pricing of his deals; in return, he obtains the pricing information from his competitors' deals. The development of price transparency in this way ensures that the market becomes deeper and more liquid. Partly as a result of Catex — and partly as a result of the other dynamics of the New Economy — the role of the broker in the insurance world is rapidly changing. Brokers are now having to provide more value-added services (such as analytical functions, consulting, and clearing) in return for fixed fees as opposed to large commissions.

PaperExchange is bringing the same price transparency to another industry that is currently heavily reliant on brokers and one where neither the seller nor the buyer really knows what a central market price should be. PaperExchange permits buyers and sellers of paper products of all grades and sizes to post expressions of interest to buy or sell at quoted prices. Buyers or sellers can then post counter-offers until a contract price is agreed. All price quotes are openly published on the web site.

Similarly, exchanges enable buyers and sellers to gauge the supply and demand at any point in time. The orders, or expressions of interest, that are posted at the exchange indicate how much people want to buy and sell and may also indicate who is buying or selling.

A B2B Exchange can thus generate transparency regarding pricing and the level of supply and demand in the market at any particular point in time.

Removing market inefficiencies

As well as expanding markets geographically, B2B Exchanges can remove market inefficiencies.

For example, in the securities markets one major inefficiency is what institutions call "market impact". This phenomenon occurs when information about a large buy or sell order leaks into the market and causes the price to move dramatically against the party trying to buy or sell. Leaks can happen when using brokers, market-makers and specialist firms. Studies by securities analysts like SEI Investments show that the largest transaction cost for an institution may not be the commission or a market-maker's spread, but this "market impact" as other traders move market prices in reaction to news about block trades. On the other hand, anonymity allows institutional investors to sell large blocks of a stock without fear that buyers will vanish and prices will fall sharply as word leaks out that the smart money is selling.

The electronic trading systems now being offered by ECNs (and which B2B Exchanges are adopting) can provide total anonymity for traders and thus remove market impact.

Instinet, the Reuters-owned electronic marketplace, has been able on its own to attract up to 20% of Nasdaq's daily volumes, based largely on its widely advertised anonymity and the ability to avoid market impact. In addition, sophisticated trading systems can allow traders to enter a large order, but only disclose a fraction of the volume to the market. As a visible order gets matched the electronic system automatically feeds the remaining volume into the order book in pre-set amounts. Again, this enables a large order to be executed with minimum market impact.

Outside of the securities industry there are plenty of existing supply chains that involve too many intermediaries, which creates inefficiencies. The National Transportation Exchange (NTE), for example, has been very successful in selling empty capacity on returning trucks to suppliers who previously had no way of accessing that haulage capacity. The suppliers get cut-price deals and the trucking companies get to sell previously unused back-haul space. NTE's web site (www.nte.net) states that *"it provides a real-time, neutral platform for member shippers who tender loads, as well as the direct service carrier members, which tender the available space capacity of their moving trucks. NTE has named its service 'The Exchange' because it enables its Members to conduct profitable business together, through a real-time marketplace setting, just like a stock exchange. Also, like a stock exchange, it has defined processes, data capture and reporting, open accessibility for its Members, interfaces to other needed technologies, and even processes transportation billing and payment with third party oversight."*

Vertical Knowledge

B2B Exchanges are being developed primarily by experienced vertical industry professionals who have seen that, with Internet technologies now being adopted by business, there is an enormous opportunity for them to leave their Industrial Age corporations and start up a B2B Exchange. Their former corporate employer would find this difficult to do because of the neutrality issue that we explain in Chapter 11. These professionals have deep knowledge of their particular industry and strong relationships with the main buyers and sellers in that vertical space.

This vertical knowledge is critical in order to build credibility for the exchange within that vertical quickly and to ensure that the exchange is tailored to suit that particular market.

Channel Conflicts for Manufacturers

As we saw in Chapter 2, a manufacturer that starts to offer its products for sale on-line can create enormous conflicts with its traditional distribution channels. Those distribution channels were developed to enable the manufacturer to achieve the maximum distribution of its products in a pre-Internet environment. The distribution channels also help the manufacturer to manage inventory levels of completed products and to store that inventory, in return for a percentage of the sales price. Where a manufacturer's loyalty to its traditional distribution channels keeps that manufacturer from selling on-line there is enormous potential for an independent third party to offer a neutral sales mechanism on-line.

B2B Exchanges are the neutral third-party market spaces that enable all manufacturers to change the way that they sell their products, without that manufacturer having to compete with its existing distribution channels.

Even when a manufacturer is able to put up its own on-line store front to sell directly it will find that a B2B Exchange is more attractive to many buyers. This is because a neutral, third-party exchange can post the store fronts of multiple manufacturers in one place — thus facilitating the buyer's search for the best product at the best price.

Impact of B2B Exchanges

B2B Exchanges are already having a dynamic impact on traditional markets. The effects are bound to multiply, like ripples in a pond, as this revolution is only just beginning. The main effects we have observed so far are:

- lower costs;
- higher potential profits for manufacturers who lower their procurement costs;
- increased depth and liquidity in a market;
- lower inventory requirements;
- greater transparency and more orderly markets;
- the elimination of geographical barriers and time zone differences; and
- removal of distribution channel blockages, such as agents and brokers which have a lock on a particular market — resulting in potential loss of jobs and/or changes in the nature of the role of traditional intermediaries.

A Who's Who

Four years ago there were no on-line B2B exchanges outside of the securities markets. Today, there are already around 100. Set out in Appendix A are detailed profiles of the following leading B2B Exchanges that we have studied in more depth:

- Catex — insurance markets (www.catex.com);
- Chemdex Corporation — chemicals (www.chemdex.com);
- CreditTrade — credit derivatives (www.credittrade.com);
- e-Chemicals — industrial chemicals (www.e-chemicals.com);
- Elinex — electricity forward contracts (www.el-in-ex.com);
- e-STEEL — steel and other metals (www.esteel.com);

- MetalSite — steel and other metals (www.metalsite.net);
- The National Transport Exchange — trucking (www.nte.net);
- PaperExchange — paper (www.paperexchange.com);
- PlasticsNet — plastics (www.plasticsnet.com); and
- TechEx — life sciences intellectual property (www.techex.com).

• • • • • • • • • • • • • •

Chapter Summary:

- *Early E-commerce was dominated by attempts to move traditional business models on-line.*
- *There are five new business models spawned by the Internet: aggregators, trading hubs, post and browse, auction markets, and automated exchanges.*
- *Each of these models is rapidly redefining business strategies and trade flows.*
- *B2B Exchanges remove market inefficiencies and rapidly expand markets geographically. For example, in the securities arena, ECNs are developing to create more efficient order execution away from traditional stock exchanges.*
- *Challenging an entrenched market with a new B2B Exchange is only possible if the new entrant can build liquidity at much lower cost. Increasingly cheap computing power and telecommunications bandwidth allow B2B Exchanges to challenge trading floors and other traditional trading networks.*
- *The low cost of getting connected, irrespective of geographical distance, enables fragmented buyers and sellers to find each other through a B2B Exchange without incurring real-world search and travel expenses or high commissions for using intermediaries.*
- *Vertical knowledge is critical in order to build credibility for the exchange within that vertical quickly and in order to ensure that the exchange is tailored to suit that particular market.*
- *Some leading examples of B2B Exchanges are Catex, Elinex, e-STEEL, MetalSite. PaperExchange, CreditTrade, TechEx, Chemdex, PaperExchange, PlasticsNet, and the National Transportation Exchange.*

Chapter 4:

"It's NOT About the Technology, Stupid!"

Although it is the technology of the Internet that is making B2B Exchanges possible, they are primarily business applications and not technological innovations. The real long-term value of a B2B Exchange to its users is greatly enhanced if the exchange is tailor-made for the specific market in which it operates — and this requires the exchange to be designed primarily from a business perspective rather than a purely technological one.

Indeed, the Internet and Web browser-based technologies are now ubiquitous, so the value of an exchange must come from the market-specific design and business solution.

Customizing the Exchange's Offering

In the physical world, the successful exchanges have been those that focus on a specific area. For example, in the securities industry the Nasdaq exchange has been successful, despite the strength of the NYSE, because it specializes in listing smaller capitalization and high-growth technology stocks that are not so welcome on the "Big Board" at the NYSE. Similarly, physical markets are tailored specifically for their users. For example, a cattle auction is held at a location that facilitates the delivery, storage and display of cattle and is held at a time that is suitable for farmers; whereas a second-hand car auction is held at a different facility and is designed specifically for car dealers. Physical auctions do not mix different products into the same program.

The on-line world is no different; users want to log into a site which is specifically designed for them and for their market, so that they can get the information or products they want as quickly as possible.

Take a look at Manheim (www.manheim.com) and their CyberLot Demo, which is an on-line second-hand car auction. The site is specifically designed for car dealers and does not mix in other products. Similarly, CattleOfferings.com is specifically designed for livestock sales and the agribusiness. The key issue here is to create a "community" which has a look, feel and functionality that all the specialized users immediately recognize. Equally important, it has to be simple, easy to use, and have low barriers to entry, that is, no new hardware, proprietary software, or other up-front costs. Fortunately, the Network, based on Internet technologies with widespread connectivity allows you to do this in the New Economy.

Securing Critical Mass

In order to kick-start the laws of increasing returns, it is very important for an exchange to build up the number of buyers and sellers that use its market space as quickly as possible.

Establishing a critical mass of users is far more important to the ultimate success of the exchange than having the most advanced technology.

Use Open, Internet-based Systems

The main technology being adopted by B2B Exchanges is TCP/IP-based systems and standards like Extensible Mark-up Language (XML) as the common protocol to define data. Use of this standard enables you to build on the Internet and browser-based applications that are now ubiquitous. It is not advisable to spend any money building a closed proprietary system, even if you think that locking users into your system will protect you from competition — that is the cul-de-sac that EDI drove into.

A good example of the power of the Internet is the Catex (www.catex.com) insurance risk B2B Exchange. Version 1 of the Catex trading and information application was built as a proprietary system using Windows NT 4.0 and required each user to have a dedicated connection, or dial-up access, to the exchange's servers. In November 1998, the exchange launched Version 2 as an open, web-based application. Immediately the system was accessible by any pre-authorized executive with a web browser on a PC with Internet access. Demonstrating the system immediately became a simple matter — instead of lugging around a heavy-duty laptop with a demo of the Version 1 system on it, a customer representative could pull up the system on the client's desktop and show them the live version. The sign-up of new subscribers has grown exponentially since they switched over to the Internet system. "It has had a dramatic impact" Frank Fortunato, the CEO of Catex, is reported as saying in an article in *Insurance Networking*. "We can deliver the product much more quickly." Anyone with Internet access and a valid user ID and password can now access the live Catex trading system on-line.

Security worries have largely been removed on the Internet with the use of user names and passwords to restrict access and the use of standard encryption methods to protect confidential information passing over the open net. Also, in the B2B market space, exchanges are able to offer authentication and tracking services for communications through an exchange's infrastructure, anonymity where applicable, and digital signatures to sign and secure digital documents.

Outsource the Technology

Throughout this book we advise the builders of B2B Exchanges to outsource the technology development. It is critical for a successful B2B Exchange to focus on its core competency — the specific industry expertise that will enable it to create the best business solution possible for that market — and let the outside technology experts build the system. A good example is the e-STEEL exchange, which partnered right at the start with Computer Services Corporation (CSC) to build the trading system. This left the management of e-STEEL free to work with the steel industry to market the exchange and get user input on the design of the system.

For the last three years, B2B Exchanges have had to build their own systems because third-party options were not available. Over the last 12 months, a rash of start ups have rushed to build and sell the technology for on-line auctions and other exchange functions. Prominent among these are Ariba and Commerce One, which offer E-commerce suites to handle on-line catalog sites — the aggregator model; Moai Technologies and OpenSite Technologies for auction-based sites; and Tradex, Optimark, Tradeum, and Mutant Technology for B2B Exchanges. As the B2B Exchange market space expands, the traditional software companies are going to expand their offerings in this area. For example, IBM already has a suite of E-commerce products, and Microsoft has also moved into the on-line auction space with an auction tool kit for its Site Server Commerce software. In addition, some of the specialist stock exchange system vendors, such as EFA Software, OM Systems and Computershare, will soon see the opportunity to re-focus their industrial strength trading and matching engines for securities onto B2B Exchange applications.

Indeed, one of the opportunities spawned by the growth of B2B Exchanges lies in the provision of technology, marketing, connectivity, content and data services, and consulting to these new companies. Forrester Research projects that the overall market for just the software that facilitates E-commerce could reach nearly $500 million by 2003.

Industry Expertise — Vertical Knowledge

B2B Exchanges need the highest level of industry specific expertise in order to gain widespread acceptance and credibility quickly within their chosen market space. It is the "kiss of death" for a start-up exchange to be directed to talk with the IT staff within the potential suppliers and buyers, rather than meeting with their senior business people, traders, the CFO and in many cases the CEO. The B2B Exchange is a business solution that requires the full endorsement of the top management and not just the approval of the technology staff. This is particularly true where the exchange is creating a paradigm shift in the way that business is done in that market space. In many cases, there is a disconnect between IT and business leaders in terms of understanding the strategic direction of the company.

However, over the past 12 months, many companies have recognized the importance of the New Economy to their company and have placed a high priority on their company's Internet strategy. Many Fortune 500 companies like GE have formed special SWAT teams of senior executives reporting directly to the CEO to address these issues. A Goldman Sachs' proprietary " GS B2B Survey 1.0", conducted in August 1999, indicates that more and more US companies are identifying the CFO as the officer who is "best equipped to answer questions" about the company's Internet strategy.

PaperExchange is chaired by Roger Stone, one of the leading luminaries of the paper industry. Roger Stone built the Stone Container Corporation into a $7.8 billion revenue company, prior to its merger with Jefferson Smurfit in late 1998. Stone Container was the largest containerboard and packaging company in the world, with 43,000 employees and operations in more than 50 countries. Jason Weiss, the CEO of PaperExchange is reported as stating that "Every CEO of every paper mill in the world knows Roger Stone and will meet with him…He'll make the mills feel comfortable with us and know that we're going to help the industry".

Frank Fortunato and Frank Sweeney, who between them have many years of experience as attorneys in the insurance industry, conceived of the Catastrophe Risk Exchange. Based on their credibility within the industry they were able to get US insurance companies to work closely with them from the inception on the design and build of the Catex trading system. This led to many ideas for design features and industry-specific functions that the technology team would not otherwise have thought of immediately.

Horizontal Trading Hubs

In July 1999, Oracle announced the launch of the "Oracle Exchange". This is one of a number of initiatives by technology companies to provide marketplaces for enterprise suppliers and purchasers to buy and sell products and services. Oracle Exchange has announced that content and related services from more than 260 companies will be available on Oracle Exchange through the Oracle Supplier Network. Oracle Supplier Network is a group of suppliers and content service providers that integrate with Oracle Strategic Procurement applications, which will populate Oracle Exchange and provide buyers with the ability to access suppliers' products and services and to buy them over the Internet. Together, Oracle Exchange and Oracle Supplier Network will enable companies to take greater advantage of the Internet's ability to reduce costs, streamline processes and capture new markets.

Also in this space are existing trading hubs like VerticalNet (www.verticalnet.com) and FreeMarkets (www.freemarkets.com). These sites build buyer and seller communities for specific industries that have not yet embraced the Internet. Sellers are given virtual storefronts to advertise their products and buyers are attracted by news, product specification information, product reviews and product recommendations. Trading hubs are moving into the provision of auction sale mechanisms, especially for large items with infrequent sales. For example, VeticalNet has auctioned three power plants in their "poweronline" vertical.

We call this model a horizontal trading hub because the companies seek to offer similar applications and support all the buyers and sellers across multiple diverse industries (or verticals). For example, VerticalNet currently operates 47 vertical communities grouped into ten sectors: advanced technologies; communications; environmental; food and packaging; food service/hospitality; healthcare; manufacturing and metals; science; and services.

One of the issues that will arise with this type of service is whether a "one size fits all" model can be successful in the B2B Exchange market space. We believe that only industry-specific sites will be successful and will gain widespread adoption within that industry. Once a community has developed in a horizontal trading hub it may migrate to a B2B Exchange that is run by experts with specialist knowledge in that vertical and which is specifically tailored for that market. In such cases the horizontal trading hubs will come to act as catalysts or incubators for subsequent specialist B2B Exchanges.

Horizontal trading hubs will flourish in niche areas, such as auctioning last year's fashions and other excess inventory, where a company is only dealing infrequently and, therefore, there is not enough critical mass to support an industry-specific site.

Diagonal Trading Hubs

Diagonal trading hubs specialize in supporting a specific type of buyer or seller, or a specific type of product category across multiple industries.

Prominent in this area is Tradeout (www.tradeout.com), a specialist trading hub for businesses to liquidate surplus inventory and idle assets. Tradeout estimates that the marketplace for businesses selling unproductive assets is worth over $300 billion per year. Currently, excess inventory and idle assets are sold globally through a variety of inefficient distribution channels. Sellers get prices less than fair market value and buyers frequently cannot locate items they want when they want them. Tradeout seeks to reduce this inefficiency by providing a central Internet-based B2B Exchange where a large universe of buyers and sellers can connect on-line.

Tradeout sells items in over 50 product categories in an auction-based, sealed-bid, or fixed-price format.

Another example of a diagonal trading hub is Shop2gether (www.shop2gether.com). Shop2gether enables small business buyers to aggregate their orders into one larger order, which is then "bid" for by multiple sellers. Shop2gether is not focused on a specific industry or vertical; rather, it is focused on the small business buyer in multiple verticals — in effect, the small business buyer is the vertical.

Diagonal trading hubs are likely to be highly successful because they are focused on providing a specific, tailored service to a particular type of buyer or seller.

• • • • • • • • • • • • • •

Chapter Summary:

- *B2B Exchanges are business applications, not IT applications.*
- *The Internet and browser-based technologies are now ubiquitous, so the value of an exchange must come from the market-specific design and business solution.*
- *Do not build a proprietary model (e.g. Catex Ver. 1.0); use the Internet (Catex Ver. 2.0).*
- *Outsource the technology (e.g. e-STEEL).*
- *Companies now sell the core technologies (e.g. Tradex and Opensite (auction markets)).*
- *B2B Exchanges need a high level of industry-specific expertise and credibility so that they can get in to see the CFO or CEO of potential members and do not get directed away to speak to the IT people.*
- *Horizontal trading hubs and technology initiatives such as the Oracle Exchange, which attempt to build business-to-business trading networks for multiple diverse industries, may just become incubators for specialized B2B Exchanges in each vertical unless they specialize in a niche, such as auctioning off excess inventory, which does not happen frequently.*
- *Diagonal trading hubs, which focus on a specific type of buyer or seller, or a specific product category across multiple markets, should be very successful.*

Part II

Anatomy of a B2B Exchange

Chapter 5:

Membership and Ownership Models

As we explained in Chapter 1, the unique feature of an exchange is that it brings multiple buyers and sellers together in a central market space and enables them to buy and sell from each other at a price that is determined in accordance with the rules of the exchange. Since an exchange represents **multiple** buyers and sellers there is a specialized approach to building a successful B2B Exchange versus a standard B2B E-commerce company.

In particular, an exchange must remain neutral and balance the competing interests of all its users. Providing an open, fair, and transparent market for all the users is a key element of an exchange's value proposition and enhances its ability to attract business.

B2B Exchanges will have some or all of the following different user groups, many of whom will have different objectives and/or interests:

- owners — that is, the shareholders;
- sellers or suppliers;
- buyers or procuring companies;
- brokers or other forms of intermediaries/infomediaries;
- listed companies (e.g. for stock exchanges);
- issuers of traded products (e.g. securitized contracts);
- data vendors and service providers;

- the general public; and
- government.

The Concept of Membership

Since an exchange has multiple buyers and sellers accessing its trading systems, it must have some form of membership structure to determine who is permitted to have access and what type of access they will have to the central market space.

This membership structure may be as simple as a subscription agreement which a potential user must complete in order to sign on — rather like new consumers can simply sign on to eBay to trade in their on-line C2C auctions. At the other end of the scale, the membership requirements may include a full set of Trading Membership Rules and Trading Regulations, which require new members to be pre-vetted and approved by the exchange. In such cases, the rules will cover the initial requirements for obtaining membership, the obligations assumed by the member, the on-going compliance requirements to be met by the member, and the system requirements for members.

The initial requirements for obtaining membership of the exchange will usually cover appropriate criteria such as:

- whether the member is fit and proper;
- relevant experience of the staff;
- creditworthiness of the firm;
- capital of the firm; and
- proper regulatory controls within the firm.

Regulating who has access to the market and how they can operate within the market is also a key element of a B2B Exchange's value proposition. For example, CreditTrade.com restricts trading access to pre-vetted financial institutions. In order to sign up as a trader you must fill in forms on the web site and then await the receipt of a user name and password, following the due diligence checks carried out by the exchange.

Stock exchanges are one of the oldest forms of formalized central markets. The first stock exchange was founded in Amsterdam in 1611. Over the years, stock exchanges have developed and refined several membership models. Our experience in dealing with traditional stock exchanges has provided us with some very important lessons in understanding the potential membership and ownership models for B2B Exchanges.

The Four Standard Models

There are essentially four common membership and ownership structures for exchanges, namely:

- ownership by one group of users — with closed membership;
- ownership by multiple user groups and with open membership;
- ownership by one or more commercial investors and with open membership; and
- ownership by government.

Owned exclusively by one group of users — closed membership

An exchange may be owned and controlled by one group of users (for example, the traders or brokers who act for buyers and sellers in the market). In this model, new trading members are required to buy an ownership stake in the exchange (often referred to as a "seat").

The advantage of this model is that the ownership group can design the market to their own particular advantage and profit. In particular, they can restrict membership through restricting who buys a "seat" or by limiting the number of seats available (thus ensuring that the price of a seat appreciates in value!). The biggest problem is that all other user groups may be disadvantaged by the owners' anti-competitive practices.

An example of this approach was called the World Insurance Network (www.worldins.com). A consortium of the largest insurance brokers set up this company in 1995, with the aim of providing E-commerce facilities to insurance and reinsurance companies. Despite spending millions of dollars on building a proprietary EDI product, the service never achieved widespread acceptance, because it was owned and controlled by six insurance brokers — which have subsequently merged to become just three large firms. The company spent those dollars in designing EDI standards and building physical networks for insurance players to communicate with one another and then discovered that with the advent of the Internet there is now one common standard and communication is no longer the issue. The company has been merged with two other EDI-based solutions called RINET and LIMNET and renamed WISe — for Worldwide Insurance E-commerce. WISe, however, is still constrained from becoming a true B2B Exchange because it is owned by the brokers and the largest insurance companies and the owners do not want WISe to compete with them in their present business space.

As the digital economy develops, it will be increasingly tempting for intermediaries, such as brokers, in all markets affected by the B2B revolution, to consider setting up their own exchange to try and protect their market position. However, as we shall demonstrate, broker-owned exchanges are no longer viable in the face of the open competition that is made possible by the Internet.

— Securities market examples —

Most old stock exchanges were set up by stockbrokers and are still exclusively owned by the brokers, for example, the New York Stock Exchange, the London Stock Exchange, and the Toronto Stock Exchange. This type of exchange operates rather like a "mutual society" or private club.

The NYSE is an example of what can happen when an exchange is owned by one group of users (in this case the broker members). The original "Buttonwood Tree" Agreement that formally constituted the NYSE on 17 May 1792 (it was named after a Buttonwood tree at 68 Wall Street under which the brokers used to meet), states as follows:

"We the subscribers, brokers for the purchase and sale of public stock do hereby solemnly promise and pledge ourselves to each other, that we will not buy or sell from this day on for any persons what-so-ever

any kind of public stock at less rate than one-quarter percent commission on the special value of, and that we give preference to each other in our negotiations."

So the brokers sought to exclude other traders and to control the prices at which stocks were bought and sold, and particularly, the price of the commissions charged by the brokers for trading on behalf of a client. A fixed commission structure effectively prevents the brokers from competing on price and denies the investing public the economic benefits of competitive market forces. In the UK, the practice of imposing minimum fixed-scale fees was cited as an anti-competitive restriction in an anti-trust case brought against the London Stock Exchange under the Restrictive Trade Practices Act of 1976. It was in part due to the fact that the NYSE acted as a private club that the US Government passed the Securities Exchange Act of 1934, which requires all National Securities Markets to be registered by the SEC. However, it was not until 1975 that the SEC finally forced the NYSE to give up its fixed commission structure. But some broker-owned stock exchanges, including the Stock Exchange of Hong Kong, still maintain fixed commissions.

Other forms of restrictive practice that are commonly carried on by a broker-owned exchange include:

- a closed system, not allowing "remote" members to have access (e.g. the Stock Exchange of Hong Kong);
- restrictions on the number of terminals and/or number of branches or offices that a member can have (e.g. the Stock Exchange of Hong Kong);
- restrictions on how many shares/seats a member can own (e.g. the NYSE); and
- weighted voting rights or restrictions on how many votes certain types of member can have (e.g. The Chicago Board of Trade).

In the 1970s, the NYSE embarked upon a decade of adjustments to its practices and governance following dramatic declines in revenues, membership (a one-third decline between 1968 and 1972), and the value of its seats. Partly on its own initiative and partly in response to pressures from the SEC, the NYSE introduced changes in its trading procedures, including limited automation and the admission of "access" members who were not required to have an ownership stake, and a removal of the fixed commission structure. The Board was reduced from 33 to 21 members, the majority of whom are now drawn from the public rather than member firms, and industry representation on the Board was also revised. Key management roles like the Chairman, CEO, and COO were turned over to professionals, outside of the membership.

In the digital revolution that is creating the New Economy, the NYSE has faced new and increasing competition from ECNs.

These electronic trading systems enable orders to bypass the NYSE and Nasdaq, and instead seek to match the orders in a central limit order book. In the face of the threat posed by these new hybrid exchanges, the NYSE claims that it cannot compete without further capital (even though it has already spent over $1 billion on technology since 1994). The NYSE now proposes to "de-mutualize", which involves a transformation from a broker-owned association into a for-profit company, and to file for its own IPO.

In the last 20 years, the anti-competitive features of broker-owned stock exchanges have become increasingly unacceptable and governments all over the world have sought to make broker-owned stock exchanges more representative of the wider public interest. As with the NYSE, the most common approach has been to require the governing body of the exchange to include a number of non-broker representatives. Sometimes, the government insists on appointing a number of government representatives. In the last five years, competitive pressures from electronic trading systems have forced all broker-owned exchanges to consider "de-mutualization" to become for-profit entities which remove all of their restrictive practices. The Bermuda Stock Exchange de-mutualized in 1992 and the Stockholm Stock Exchange de-mutualized and went public in 1993. The Australian Stock Exchange went public in 1998 and now the NYSE, Nasdaq, Toronto and London Stock Exchanges are all talking about going public.

Owned by multiple users — open membership

An alternative approach is to start with wider ownership, which represents all of the users of the exchange. Under this model, the application for membership, or ability to trade on the exchange, is not linked to an ownership stake and new memberships are on a non-discriminatory basis. This means that a member does not have to own a seat, but rather has a license to trade on the exchange and to use the facilities of the exchange. This license may be transferable by a member, or the exchange may insist that new members join the exchange directly so that membership rights are non-transferable.

The advantage of this approach is the ability to balance the competing interests of each user group. The disadvantage is that it can take a long time to get all these potentially disparate groups to work together.

— Securities market examples —

The open membership model is the approach that has been adopted in many newer stock exchanges (particularly in emerging markets, which have the benefit of starting with a clean sheet). In the last ten years, most new stock exchanges have been set up by non-brokers, with the investors opening up trading membership of the exchange to everyone who meets the requirements of the exchange. Examples of this include:

- The Bermuda Stock Exchange (BSX). The BSX was "de-mutualized" in 1992 by the creation of a for-profit company. Membership was opened up and "de-coupled" from ownership.
- The Stockholm Stock Exchange (SSE) was de-mutualized in 1993 and was owned by multiple user groups until 1998 when the OM Gruppen purchased it (see below).
- Luxembourg Stock Exchange. The Exchange is a public company with wide share ownership that distributes surpluses to shareholders as dividends.
- The National Stock Exchange of India (owned by a group of financial institutions). The NSE was set up with the blessing of government to counteract the anti-competitive practices adopted

by the Bombay Stock Exchange over a number of years. By implementing a fully-electronic dealing system with equal access from all the main cities (by way of satellite-linked terminals), the NSE was able to surpass Bombay as the leading stock exchange in India, by volume, within 18 months of its launch.

The SSE is an interesting example of this model. In 1993, the SSE transformed itself from a traditional old broker-owned exchange into a public company owned as to 50% by the broker members and 50% by the listed companies. Shares in the Stockholm Exchange Company were then made available for members of the public to buy. The move to privatized ownership was seen as particularly important to achieving faster decision-making and responding more effectively to the market. The SSE's first act as a private company was to allow remote membership and direct execution of orders from other cities.

These strategic initiatives have succeeded by almost every measure. The market has flourished, with market capitalization increasing five times and trading volumes increasing 20 times, since 1990. Trading fees have been cut by more than half and entry fees for members by two-thirds. The Exchange has also attracted more liquidity, in fact, 90% of companies inter-listed on the NYSE now trade 90% of their volume in Stockholm. The SSE has also succeeded in expanding its international presence as many members trade remotely. The SSE is also the first stock exchange to receive the coveted ISO 9001 certification.

In 1998, the OM Gruppen that operated several securities exchanges, including a traded options market called OM Stockholm, bought the SSE. On 1 July 1999, the Stockholm Stock Exchange and OM Stockholm merged to establish the OM Stockholm Exchange, with the activities of the Stockholm Stock Exchange and OM Stockholm combined in this newly-incorporated entity.

Owned by one or more benign commercial investors

Under this model, the exchange is set up and operated by one benign investor or a group of investors and is run totally on a commercial basis, for profit. As above, under this model the membership, or ability to trade on the exchange, is not linked to the ownership, and new memberships are available to new members on an open access, non-discriminatory basis without the requirement to purchase a seat.

This model is the one most prevalent in the establishment of most B2B Exchanges over the last four years.

Good examples are Catex, CreditTrade, e-Chemicals, Elinex, PaperExchange, PlasticsNet, National Transportation Exchange, and TechEx.

PlasticsNet's story is typical of the funding history in the development of many independent, third-party B2B Exchanges. In early 1994, Tim and Nick Stojka discovered a way that the Internet might be used to streamline the supply chain processes in the plastics industry and they began to explore the concept for PlasticsNet. Sons of the founder of Fast Heat, a supplier to the plastics industry, the Stojka brothers grew up in the plastics business and understood industry practices. But they also recognized the problems the Internet could solve. Based in Chicago, the brothers established CommerX (www.commerx.com) as a private company and launched PlasticsNet (www.plasticsnet.com) in September 1995.

PlasticsNet was initially funded by CommerX as a benign commercial investor. A second round of financing raised funding from the Internet Capital Group. PlasticsNet is now in the process of raising a third round of financing. The brothers now claim that PlasticsNet's site is the first electronic commerce center for the $390 billion per annum US plastics industry. Since March 1999, the site has been evolving from a trade community and sourcing guide for the plastics industry into a fully-fledged marketplace with complete E-commerce capabilities. CommerX is now in the process of establishing similar exchanges in other related vertical spaces.

— Securities market examples —

In the securities markets, the best examples of this model are:

- Instinet. The largest and oldest ECN in the US, which is wholly-owned by Reuters PLC and which provides anonymous order matching.

- The Arizona Stock Exchange (www.azx.com). An electronic auction market set up and run by a group of private investors.
- Tradepoint Stock Exchange (www.tradepoint.co.uk). An electronic dealing system set up in London by a group of private investors, listed on the Vancouver Stock Exchange and now owned by a consortium of large broker-dealers including Morgan Stanley, J P Morgan and Instinet and the Archipelago ECN. Tradepoint currently trades UK equities, but aims to become a pan-European ECN with trading in the shares of all the top European companies.
- The Stockholm Stock Exchange is wholly-owned by OM Gruppen. OM Gruppen is listed on the SSE.
- The Deutsche Börse. Over the past decade, the Frankfurt Exchange (FWB) has transformed itself into Europe's fastest-growing exchange. In 1993, the Deutsche Börse AG (DB) was founded. DB runs the FWB and the German Futures Exchange (DTB). It is majority owned by the German banks, and the country's seven other regional exchanges collectively hold a minority share of the new entity.

Owned by government

Where a B2B Exchange is perceived as providing a significant public benefit the government may be tempted to assert a national interest ingredient to the development of such a market within their jurisdiction. For example, if MetalSite or e-STEEL develops as a dominant exchange for the determination of price in respect of steel products worldwide, then the major steel-producing countries in Asia may decide that they should establish competing steel exchanges in their own countries.

— Securities market examples —

There is now a universal recognition that securities markets play a crucial role in mobilizing domestic capital, attracting foreign capital, and allocating scarce resources to the most productive uses. The central role of a securities market within the economy has led governments to seek to control the operations of the stock exchange. Initially this involved an emphasis on the governing body of the exchange, with a requirement for non-broker or government representation. More recently, governments have sought to have an ownership interest in the national stock exchange. Examples of this model include:

- The Taiwan Stock Exchange (government 39%; brokers, listed companies, and the public 61%). The public sector shareholdings are freely transferable and the stock exchange distributes surpluses as dividends.
- The Cayman Islands Stock Exchange (www.csx.com.ky) which is 100%-owned by the Government.
- The Channel Islands Stock Exchange (www.cisx.ci) which is 100%-owned by the Government.

Where the government has an ownership interest in a stock exchange it may also grant that exchange a statutory monopoly. This has the advantage of removing competitive threats in that jurisdiction. On the other hand, if the exchange is given a monopoly, it raises concerns that the securities market may not remain competitive, particularly in today's global economy in which countries are competing to attract a limited supply of foreign capital.

The "Broker Dilemma"

New B2B exchanges that are not owned by the brokers in a market and which adopt an open membership structure may face the dilemma of whether to include traditional intermediaries and middlemen, such as brokers, in their new market space or whether to exclude them from membership.

Where tiers of distributors, resellers and/or brokers dominate a traditional market, the Internet offers the opportunity to "disintermediate" many of them and enable buyers and sellers to transact business directly with each other through the on-line exchange. The exchange may therefore be tempted to refuse to allow such players to be members of the exchange. In the 1970s, a group of enterprising insurance executives decided to set up a fully-electronic Risk Exchange, called REX, to enable companies to buy insurance from primary insurers without using a costly broker in the middle (a sort of early B2B version of Geico Direct). Because their main objective was to "disintermediate" the brokers, they decided to refuse membership to all insurance brokers. You probably haven't heard of REX because it failed miserably. The insurance brokers had more market power than the founders imagined as they were able to effectively direct insurers not to use the system and/or persuaded the insurers to continue using their familiar brokers.

The alternative approach is to embrace the brokers and other middlemen, but to ensure that the central, on-line market space is designed in a neutral way that does not favor or advantage the brokers.

Where the traditional intermediaries have dominated the existing market, it is critical for a proposed B2B Exchange in that vertical to co-opt the brokers into the system so that they bring their deal flow and liquidity to the central market space.

One example of how the exchange can accommodate brokers is to design the system so that a broker's posting or orders are only visible to potential buyers or sellers and cannot be seen by other competing brokers. This encourages the brokers to use the exchange in order to benefit from all the advantages of a centralized, on-line market but without having to let their competitors see any of their deal flow.

• • • • • • • • • • • • •

Chapter Summary:

• *Unlike E-commerce companies, B2B Exchanges have multiple user groups — buyers, sellers, brokers, infomediaries, listed issuers, the public, etc.*

• *An exchange must remain neutral and balance the competing interests of all its users. Providing an open, fair and transparent market for all the users is a key element of an exchange's value proposition and enhances the exchange's ability to attract business.*

• *Exchanges must embrace the concept of membership in addition to ownership.*

• *Mutual Society Model — owned by one user group — problems with anti-competitive practices (e.g. the NYSE). Now broker-owned stock exchanges like the NYSE want to go public due to competition from electronic markets like ECNs.*

• *Benign investor model. For-profit, open membership (e.g. PlasticsNet).*

• *Government-owned models.*

• *Exchanges must regulate their own members' activities.*

• *The importance of credibility, integrity and liquidity for exchanges.*

• *New exchanges may be tempted to exclude intermediaries. But where the traditional intermediaries have dominated the existing market, it is critical for a proposed B2B Exchange in that vertical to co-opt the brokers into the system so that they bring their deal flow and liquidity to the central market space.*

Chapter 6:

Trading Models

The Internet has enabled a number of different trading models for B2B Exchanges. Indeed, on-line, business-to-business trading may be the first business model that truly exploits the unique characteristics of the Internet. We believe that the centralized market spaces created by B2B Exchanges are the killer application which will drive increased use of the Internet by businesses.

Earlier Internet business models have tended to replicate in cyberspace the dynamics of the physical world. The ability to buy a fixed-price plane ticket or a book on-line is attractive to us because it is convenient, and we get immediate access to a relatively larger universe of similar fixed-price goods on the Internet. But, like the consumer in the bookstore or at the airline counter, the on-line consumer at Amazon.com or Travelocity.com must accept a fixed price, or click away.

By exploiting the unique nature of the Internet, a B2B Exchange's on-line centralized trading space facilitates the connecting of buyers with sellers and the generation of "dynamic pricing".

Dynamic Pricing Establishes Market Prices

By bringing together all the potential buy and sell orders at any particular time and letting those competing offers set the highest price or the price which maximizes the amount sold, the exchange's price can truly be called the market price at that particular point in time.

Dynamic pricing — through competitive bidding and auction systems — is one of the most exciting features of B2B Exchanges and represents a key component of the revolutionary nature of B2B Internet commerce.

The Four New Trading Models

As we saw in Chapter 3, the Internet has spawned five new business models for on-line exchanges. These five business models encompass the following four trading methods:

- fixed pricing (e.g. catalog aggregators);
- one-on-one negotiation;
- auction markets;
  - seller-driven auctions;
  - buyer-driven (or reverse) auctions; and
- electronic auto-execution systems (two-way auctions).

Business Model	Trading Mechanism
Aggregators	Fixed prices. Moving towards auctions.
Trading hubs	Fixed prices and some buyer-driven (reverse)auctions.
Post and browse	Individual deals. One-on-one negotiated terms and prices, called the "over-the-counter" market in the securities industry.
Auction markets	Dynamic pricing. Seller-driven and buyer-driven (reverse) auctions.
Fully-automated exchanges	Dynamic pricing. Automated matching of orders, continuous auction markets.

A good B2B Exchange will also facilitate the listing of goods or services for sale, the exchange of information, the ability of members to negotiate with each other on price and other features as well as the ability, eventually, for members to execute a transaction on-line. The Internet also allows buyers and sellers to trade directly, bypassing traditional intermediaries, which can lower the costs for both parties.

A B2B Exchange's trading space is global in reach, offers significant convenience, and facilitates a sense of community by fostering direct buyer and seller communication.

Fixed prices: Catalog aggregators

Catalog aggregators aim to provide a one-stop shopping venue for procurement by companies. The aggregator streamlines purchasing by aggregating the product catalogs of many suppliers in one place (a web site) and in one format. The parts and products displayed on-line in such a site can number in the hundreds of thousands.

Instead of phoning and faxing multiple potential suppliers, these sites enable a procurement manager to obtain all of the product and pricing information he needs in one centralized site.

Only a neutral, independent site that is operated by a third party is able to bring multiple competing sellers together in this way. And buyers will only trust the information on the site if the aggregator is neutral and independent.

This model works best for the sale of low-priced items that are bought frequently, but in small quantities. Accordingly, it does not make sense to negotiate the price on every trade. The price of products on a catalog aggregator tends to be fairly static — prices are as stated in the supplier's catalog.

Catalog aggregators can expand their offering by enabling a procurement manager to issue a "request for quotes" to a short list of suppliers through the web site, for large orders or items which are not standard. For example, e-Chemicals has enhanced its system through a joint venture with Yellow Freight that handles the logistics of delivering products to buyers. e-Chemicals takes delivery of the products from the supplier and forwards them on to the buyer. Yellow Freight's services enable the buyer to check the order status on-line.

Examples: Chemdex, e-Chemicals, PlasticsNet, many of VerticalNet's trading hubs

One-on-one negotiations: post and browse

The most basic form of active trading is the post and browse approach. This is primarily a structured, and in many cases sophisticated, Bulletin Board on the Web where authorized members of the exchange can post expressions of interest to buy or sell or exchange goods or services. In this model, the price is negotiated for each transaction through a one-on-one negotiation.

This model is essentially similar to an Internet-based meeting room, but because the exchange pre-qualifies users before they are authorized to post or to respond to postings on the Bulletin Board, it is really a private members' room into which only certain types of people are allowed.

Just like a private members' room, the post and browse function creates a virtual community — a group of people who are interested in buying or selling a particular product and who can make a connection through the Bulletin Board.

Most post and browse systems provide a main screen that lists members' postings by one or more categories (for example, by product category or by date of posting, etc.) and allocates each posting a unique number.

Catex is based on a post and browse model. In the insurance industry, each contract is individually negotiated based on the unique risk features of the properties, goods or financial exposures that are being insured. It is, therefore, very difficult to prepare standard contracts that can be traded automatically. Instead, the parties need to exchange a lot of information about each other (for example, credit information in respect of the insured and underwriting history in respect of the insurer, together with details about the risks to be covered). This necessitates business-to-business negotiations on every contract. The post and browse feature on Catex enables users to post expressions of interest to buy insurance (that is, cede a risk to an insurer) or sell insurance (that is, offer to assume a particular risk). Based on the information posted, the users are able to establish a connection and proceed to negotiate a price and an insurance contract between themselves. CreditTrade provides a similar type of post and browse for institutional players who wish to trade credit default swaps. The parties "meet" anonymously through the post and browse board and then enter into detailed contract negotiations.

PaperExchange enables a buyer to respond to a price posted on the screen by a seller. The buyer can either accept the price offered or post a counter-bid. The seller can then either accept this counter-offer or post a revised price for the buyer to accept or counter-bid on.

Around this basic match-making functionality the exchange must provide other services in order to attract new users and to support existing users of the system.

These services include:

- A method, or methods, for members to communicate with each other in order to respond to a posting or negotiate the terms of a deal — together with a directory of all users and a method to authenticate messages passed through the system.
- Information about the products on offer which help buyers to understand what is being offered for sale and forums which enable buyers to exchange information and pass on recommendations about products.
- Post-trade information in respect of deals done through the exchange which helps buyers and sellers to understand what the market price for a particular product or service is at any point in time.
- Document management services to enable the parties to post, send and receive trade and supporting documents or to prepare contractual documents on-line. This feature enables users to cut down on the use of fax machines and courier companies for

exchange of documents and can provide a secure service with authentication and an audit trail of what documents have been exchanged.

- The legal framework within which the members can trade with legal certainty and with complete trust.
- Security and privacy; often these services will be provided with different levels of security or privacy available as required by different users.

Communications between users of the post and browse feature are critical. The most obvious method is to provide e-mail services. This enables the exchange to build up a "Rolodex" of the important users in the industry.

However, many users of an exchange will want to retain anonymity, at least in the early stages of a negotiation, in order to avoid showing their hand too early.

B2B Exchanges can facilitate this in several ways. The first way is to provide for anonymous e-mail. For example, Catex advertises the fact that it provides an "A-Mail" function that enables users to exchange e-mail without disclosing who they are. An additional neat feature of Catex's A-Mail is that, once a user is ready to disclose who they are, they can check a box that provides for disclosure of the user's identity. If both parties are using aliases, then the system will only disclose one party's name to the other if they have BOTH checked the box and approve of simultaneous disclosure of identities. CreditTrade also provides anonymous broker channels which enable a user to make a connection with another user without revealing their identity (until they are both ready to do so).

PaperExchange does not reveal the names of a buyer or seller to any party until they have agreed on a price and quantity through the exchange's anonymous bidding system.

Additional communication channels can be provided by collaborative software applications such as NetMeeting from Microsoft, which enable members to work together on a document or view a presentation, whilst exchanging real-time conversations on-line.

One area in which post and browse exchanges tend not to get involved is settlement and clearing. Because each trade is individually negotiated between members, the exchange will usually require the members to sort out the transfer of payment and delivery of the goods or services between themselves, without the exchange standing in the middle in any way. However, the exchange can add to its value proposition by introducing back-office functions that support invoicing, accounting and accurate settlement reports. For example, MetalSite and PlasticsNet enable members to plug their back-office systems into the exchange's systems. PaperExchange also offers a "clearing" process and will guarantee payments by certain buyers whose creditworthiness has been approved in advance, which is a value-added service.

Post and browse exchanges are relatively easy to implement, which makes them vulnerable to competitors, and they must quickly evolve more sophisticated trading models (e.g. auctions) if they wish to enhance their value proposition for the members.

Examples: Catex, CreditTrade, PaperExchange

Dynamic pricing: auction markets

The auction format is one approach that is likely to become increasingly popular for B2B Exchanges, as it enhances efficiency while maximizing the return for the buyer or the seller. In addition, an auction market concentrates or pools the liquidity (that is, all the buy and sell orders) into one specific point in time when the auction closes.

The ability of multiple buyers and sellers to collectively set prices for a wide range of goods and services creates a dynamic pricing model and represents a radical departure from the older, fixed-price model of the Industrial Age.

Until the Internet took off, businesses were forced to pay fixed prices for standardized goods because one-on-one negotiation was inefficient for centralized, mass producers. But now, the advent and growth of

Internet-based auctions provides the opportunity for a more efficient, more satisfying relationship between buyers and sellers. In an auction, buyers bid no more than they are willing to pay (and have no excuses for overpaying); and sellers who ask for too high a price (by posting a high minimum bid) must soon lower their price, or choose not to sell. Buyers have increased selection, more convenience, and the opportunity to pay less. Sellers have a larger market and the opportunity to charge more.

On-line auctions developed initially in the C2C space as a highly efficient way to facilitate person-to-person transactions (for example, the sale of antiques or memorabilia between individuals on eBay). The ability to sell one-of-a-kind, previously owned items in the pre-Internet, physical world was very difficult. Consumers trying to sell one-of-a-kind products were often constrained to a small, localized marketplace in which to locate potential buyers (for example, flea markets, garage sales, local classifieds, etc.). Now companies like eBay have been able to offer consumers a way to offer their personal items for sale on a global basis through on-line auctions.

Seller-driven auctions

In this approach the seller drives the auction. The seller lists the item to sell and multiple buyers submit upward price bids for the designated item or service. This format is utilized by eBay and tends to lead to an increase in the price bid as time extends and the close of the auction approaches (see graph). This works well for sellers who can get the highest price for their goods while using the Internet to maximize their reach to a large number of potential buyers. This facilitates efficient market pricing. This system works especially well for items that are unique and differentiated, but which are relatively simple to describe and understand.

The system is less favorable to buyers, because there is no negotiation between the buyer and the seller — just a competition between all the buyers.

Seller-driven auction

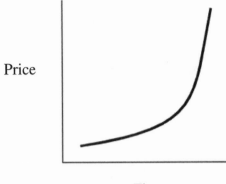

Price

Time

In the B2B space, this type of auction is particularly good for liquidating surplus goods. In this area the goods have a well-known first-run market price, but are expected to sell at a substantial discount. The auction mechanism replaces the traditional liquidation brokers who only offer "fire sale" prices. Forrester Research have noticed that as companies use seller-driven auctions more frequently as their standard way of liquidating surplus goods, they are able to move surplus inventory more quickly and thus reduce their overall inventory holding costs. MetalSite is a good example of a B2B Exchange that provides auctions to clear surplus materials for the steel industry.

Buyer-driven (or reverse) auctions

In this approach, the auction format is inverted, with buyers specifying the items they want and multiple sellers competing for the buyer's business in a downward price auction.

This approach clearly favors the buyers, especially if there are multiple sellers able to offer items that come close to meeting the buyer's requirements.

In this type of auction, the price tends to fall over time as you approach the close of the auction (see graph).

Buyer-driven or reverse auction

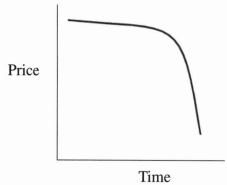

Price

Time

This is the model adopted by the horizontal trading hubs, such as FreeMarkets and VerticalNet, that facilitate procurement of supplies by companies. FreeMarkets OnLine operates real-time, business-to-business on-line auctions for companies buying custom industrial components electronics, and commodities such as coal and steel. It uses its BidWare software to link buyers with sellers in timed, reverse auctions in which suppliers place bids to fill an order. The company's clients have included Caterpillar, FirstEnergy, and the Commonwealth of Pennsylvania. FreeMarkets collects fees for conducting the auctions and sometimes takes a percentage of what the buyers save. The company organizes and conducts real-time interactive competitive bidding events that enable large buying organizations to purchase industrial materials and components at true market prices. In 1998 alone, FreeMarkets created on-line markets for over $1 billion worth of industrial materials and components.

The items on which bids are to be placed are grouped into "lots" and then sufficient suppliers are included to ensure there is competitive bidding. FreeMarkets pre-vets the suppliers to ensure that they are acceptable to the buyer and provides the potential suppliers with full details of the items that are being sought (for example, the purchaser's quality requirements). The purchaser is not obliged to accept the lowest bid or to switch from their incumbent supplier. During an on-line auction the suppliers remain anonymous to one another, but they can see competing price bids in real time. The buyer can see both the identity and current bid of each supplier. Auctions typically last between one and three hours.

Another good example of this economic model is Shop2gether. Shop2gether enables small business buyers to aggregate their orders for common items such as office furniture and office equipment. At a pre-set time the aggregation of similar orders is closed and then a number of suppliers are able to bid on that one large contract.

The attraction of this format for business-to-business transactions is that it can substantially reduce a company's procurement costs. However, it can only work for items that can be clearly described to the sellers and for which there are plenty of potential suppliers.

Both buyer- and seller-driven auction formats will become increasingly popular, due to the scale, reach, interactive, and real-time attributes afforded by the Internet. We believe that many diverse industries will take advantage of these basic advantages and apply them to B2B Exchanges.

One novel application of the reverse auction that we believe is bound to develop is on-line bidding between reinsurance underwriters for property catastrophe programs. As we outlined above, the wholesale reinsurance industry does not yet have "commoditized" products as each contract is negotiated individually. In the case of property catastrophe programs, a primary insurer with large property exposures — for example USAA in Florida — will seek to pass on some of that risk to a reinsurance company, for example XL MidOcean Re in Bermuda. Such property catastrophe reinsurance contracts are only negotiated once a year and remain in force until the following year. The present market practice is for the primary insurer to engage a broker (for a large commission) who assists by preparing full details of the property risks to be reinsured. The broker then submits those details (usually by fax and courier mail) to a pre-selected group of reinsurance underwriters and invites a sealed bid or quotation to be returned by a set date. None of the selected underwriters knows what other reinsurers have bid, and none of them gets the chance to adjust their bids over the time period.

In the near future, an on-line B2B Exchange like Catex, or maybe a horizontal trading hub like FreeMarkets, will offer to run this bidding process as a reverse auction. Each underwriter will be able to see the bids made by their competitors on a web site (anonymously, of course), and will have the ability to adjust their bid downward as the auction time expires.

The result of such competitive bidding on-line is likely to be lower premium rates for the primary insurer buying the program and significantly reduced commissions for the broker involved.

B2B Exchanges offering auction markets are also providing clearing and settlement services. Some sites help the sellers to link their back-office systems to the exchange in order to facilitate real-time inventory checks and fully integrated accounting. Chemdex, which provides a B2B Exchange for scientific research materials, enables suppliers to link into their systems in this way. The B2B auction exchange should also provide invoicing and credit facilities to encourage businesses to join.

Examples: FreeMarkets, Shop2gether, Tradeout

Dynamic pricing: electronic auto-execution systems

Also emerging quickly are electronic trading systems that can automatically match buyers and sellers on a continuous basis and thus create real-time, dynamic pricing. **In effect such systems are continuous two-way auctions where the seller offers to sell (the ask) and the buyer offers to buy (the bid).** The bid and ask offers must either have a fixed (that is, a limit) price or be priced at "market" (that is, at the best price offered on the other side of the market at that precise point in time). The system checks when an order is received to see if it can be immediately matched against an equal, but opposite, order already in the system. If it cannot be matched, the new order is stored in the system awaiting an equal and opposite offer to arrive.

It is usual for such systems to give first priority to orders which have the best price (the lowest ask and the highest bid order) and for orders with an equal price to be ranked strictly based on time of receipt by the trading engine — what is called "price-over-time priority". These systems therefore provide a central "limit order book" system which allows members to trade on an anonymous, equal and fair (first come, first served) basis. Auto-matching systems provide real-time prices and enable fast trading.

Limit order book systems are only effective if you have:

- standardized or "commoditized" products which are identical (e.g. securities or securitized contracts); or
- high liquidity (i.e. lots of competing bid and ask orders flowing into the order book).

If there is little liquidity in the product, then a member's limit order is unlikely to be able to find an immediate match in the system and it will sit in the order book waiting for a matching order to come in. For every second that the limit order sits out in the order book, the buyer or seller may be cruelly exposed to changes in the fair market price for the item (because that order can be automatically executed against at any time until he cancels it). This makes traders use a "fill or kill" approach whereby they enter an order at a limit price, but remove the order immediately if it is not instantly matched in the order book. (Many electronic trading systems provide a special "FOK" order type which automatically flushes the order if it does not match.)

Fill or kill orders reduce the number of orders in the central order book at any one time and thereby reduce the chances of another order being matched immediately — a vicious downward spiral that intensifies the lack of liquidity. On the other hand, a liquid market (such as the Nasdaq or NYSE stock markets) would be considerably enhanced by a central limit order system because trades are executed quickly at a low execution cost and with buyers and seller orders being matched directly at the price they offered. In highly liquid and volatile markets it is important to maintain the anonymity of buyers and sellers, as the buyer's or seller's identity could significantly affect market prices — so-called market impact, and (as we saw in Chapter 2) electronic trading systems are ideally suited for anonymous trading.

— Securities market examples —

Buyers and sellers, in a centralized location, operating according to the laws of supply and demand, are the key elements of any auction market system for the trading of stocks.

Indeed, central limit order book systems have been prevalent in securities markets outside of the US for the last 15 years. The rapid growth of ECNs in the US in the last two years is due solely to the attractions of a central limit order book system in a highly liquid market. It is interesting to note that the members of Nasdaq have consistently resisted the introduction of a central limit order book on Nasdaq — perhaps out of a fear that it would substantially erode the market-makers' profits.

The Bermuda Stock Exchange launched a fully-automatic trading system in 1998. The BSX system is called the Bermuda Electronic Securities Trading (BEST) system. BEST is a state-of-the-art trading system so it is a good example of what auto-execution, trading systems can offer. BEST operates as follows:

Pre-trading: During this period, orders can be entered, but they are not immediately processed. The purpose of the pre-trading period is to allow for price discovery of all existing orders.

Main trading: immediately at the start of the main trading session there is an "opening" of the market. During the opening the market determines the opening prices by selecting the price for each security at which the greatest number of shares will trade at the open. If the volume at two different prices would be the same, the system selects the price at which the least volume of unmatched orders will exist. If there is an order imbalance at the opening price, the system automatically allocates the executions based on the time the order was received.

The opening is fully automatic and takes less than a few seconds — thereafter the market is open for continuous trading until close of day.

During the main trading session, members may enter orders at any time and the system seeks to match any new orders with the orders already queued in the system on a strict price-over-time priority basis. If an immediate match for a bid/ask order is not available, the order is queued with the best price having priority and orders with the same price being queued in order of the time of receipt by the trading engine.

Sorting according to price/time priority ensures that bid orders with the highest limit price take precedence over buy orders with lower price limits. Vice versa, an ask order with a lower limit price takes precedence over an order with a higher limit price. In the event that there are two equally matched orders, the first order received takes precedence over the other.

Post-trading: After the market closes, orders are not accepted, processed or matched. Time-restricted orders are purged from the system, and any "Good Till Cancelled" orders are automatically carried over to the next trading session. The last trade in a security's primary market determines the closing price of a security, whether the trade is made on the same day or before.

BEST supports the creation of multiple markets within the same system and supports the trading of fixed income and equity securities. The system can operate continuous trading, periodic auctions and call-over markets. The system supports a variety of order types including market, limit, fill-or-kill, etc. Many features of the system, such as the auction mode, the priority of orders, and the hours of trading are all customizable through a simple parameter-driven administration program.

B2B Exchanges with fully-electronic trading systems must provide clearing and settlement services in order to preserve a market's integrity. Since trading is anonymous and executed automatically, it is not practical to have trades being unwound or failing to settle on a regular basis. This means that the exchange has to ensure that settlement happens. In securities markets this has led to the development of central clearing and depository companies that handle the settlement process and often provide a trade guarantee to trading members.

Successful B2B Exchanges will also have to address clearing and settlement issues. In some cases, exchanges may have to take physical delivery of the products sold and handle the logistics of delivering them to the buyer.

Advanced "Neural" Networks

As we move forward, more advanced trading systems will be developed. In the securities area, OptiMark Technologies, Inc. have developed a matching system that seeks to enable dealers to express to a secure computer their full trading interest across a continuous range of prices and quantities. The central computers then use patented algorithms to provide a sequential allocation of trades between buyers and sellers at different prices based upon a measure of mutual satisfaction. The main advantage of this system is that it enables a dealer to achieve more executions without having to expose his full hand to the market, therefore avoiding the hidden costs of market impact.

In the B2B Exchange world, trading systems will evolve that allow users to factor in a whole range of variable items on which they wish to seek satisfaction in addition to just price and quantity. For example, a procuring company is concerned about quality of product, delivery times and cost of delivery in addition to pure purchase cost per unit. These systems will probably adopt "fuzzy" logic based on neural network technology. Companies like OptiMark, Tradex, and Tradeum are currently working on such systems.

Lack of Human Interaction

One common criticism of electronic trading systems, especially from older floor traders in the securities markets, is the belief that computers remove all human interaction from the process.

There is no doubt that the buzz on a physical trading floor can sometimes be palpable — especially in the crowd around a trading post where breaking news is creating great excitement in a particular product or stock. However, there are ways of minimizing this loss. The first is to add features to the system that are analogs of the physical experience. For example, the trading system can tell you how many other dealers are currently monitoring a particular product or stock at that time — thus creating the equivalent of the crowd feeling around a particular trading post. Secondly, an on-line exchange can add various community services around the trading system, see Chapter 13, which help to increase the level of human interaction between the traders in that market and thus generate the same sense of community that physical floor traders develop amongst themselves.

In addition, a B2B Exchange should not underestimate the high level of customer support that is required in the early stages in order to persuade existing corporations to switch the way they do business.

Even after a company joins a B2B Exchange, the exchange must provide a full-time trading desk support function which provides human interaction in the form of encouragement to use, and hand holding in how to use, the exchange's centralized market systems.

The Panic Button

All exchanges should provide their members with a mechanism whereby they can withdraw all of their bids and orders from the exchange's system in one go. In BEST this takes the form of a function called "Cancel Orders Globally" which enables the cancellation of all outstanding orders through the click of just one button. This button gives the users absolute comfort that they can get out of the centralized, automated market as quickly as they can put down the phone in their off-line market.

● ● ● ● ● ● ● ● ● ● ● ● ●

Chapter Summary:

- *We believe that the centralized market spaces created by B2B Exchanges are the killer application which will drive increased use of the Internet by businesses.*
- *Trading models for B2B Exchanges include catalog aggregators; post and browse; auction markets; and continuous auto-execution systems.*
- *Catalog aggregators must be neutral, independent sites that are operated by a third party in order to be able to bring multiple competing sellers together and for the buyers to trust the information on the site.*
- *Just like a private members' room, a post and browse function creates a virtual community — a group of people who are interested in buying or selling a particular product and who can make a connection through a web-based Bulletin Board.*
- *Auction sites can provide seller-driven auctions (for example, the auctions run on eBay), or buyer-driven auctions in which suppliers bid competitively for a procurement contract.*
- *The ability of multiple buyers and sellers to collectively set prices for a wide range of goods and services represents a radical departure from the older, fixed-price model of the Industrial Age.*
- *Both buyer- and seller-driven auction formats will become increasingly popular, especially due to the scale, reach, interactive, and real-time attributes afforded by the Internet. We believe that many diverse industries will capitalize on these basic advantages and apply them in B2B Exchanges.*
- *Auto-execution systems only work if there are standardized products which are identical (for example, securities or securitized contracts) and high liquidity (that is, lots of competing bid and ask orders flowing into the order book).*
- *Sophisticated auto-execution systems (like BEST in Bermuda) should support multiple markets, multiple security types, and multiple auction modes, and be customizable through parameter-driven administration.*

- *In the future, trading systems will use "fuzzy" logic to allow traders to input multiple variables in addition to just price and quantity.*
- *All exchanges should provide traders with a global trade cancel function — like a panic button.*

Chapter 7:

Strategic Partnership Models

As Kevin Kelly points out in his excellent book *New Rules for the New Economy*, the New Economy "..favors intangible things — ideas, information, and relationships". Forming the right relationships at the start-up of a new B2B Exchange is critical in the way that the exchange will develop, and how quickly it can develop.

Elsewhere in this book, we emphasize the paramount importance of having industry-specific expertise (vertical knowledge) on board at the beginning and of emphasizing sales, marketing, and customer service. That is the core competency on which the B2B Exchange must focus. Outside of that, it is possible to obtain all of the other ingredients of a good B2B Exchange pie through relationships with key strategic partners.

In addition, B2B Exchanges must partner with key suppliers, commerce communities and information providers in order to be able to scale up quickly.

800-Pound Gorillas as Partners

In every industry vertical there are some companies that control the lion's share of the business and which are the market leaders. These firms command the respect of the other players in that vertical and are the "800-pound gorillas" in that industry.

A B2B Exchange needs to achieve "buy-in" from one or more of these gorillas in order to dominate that vertical and to gain sufficient credibility to persuade the others to follow.

For example, in the case of MetalSite, the exchange is part owned by three steel mills; $4.5 billion LTV Steel Inc., $1.5 billion Wierton Steel Corp., and $450 million Steel Dynamics Inc. Similarly, Chemdex decided to accept a 10% investment from VWR, a substantial off-line supplier of life science products, in order to secure their involvement in the Chemdex exchange.

Neutrality Issues

Clearly, the introduction of key industry players can impact the perceived neutrality of the exchange, if the "gorilla's hug" is too tight. To counteract any perceived bias, the exchange must develop and maintain a strong, independent advisory board that can act as a counter-weight to the purely commercial interests of the industry partners.

Metalsite is now facing competition from e-STEEL, which launched in early September 1999. In order to differentiate itself from MetalSite, the e-STEEL exchange is emphasizing its neutrality and independence from the large steel mill owners. e-STEEL's web site states:

"e-STEEL is a true marketplace for the exchange of steel on the Internet. Like other true markets, e-STEEL is neutral, does not own any of the products transacted on the system, and is not affiliated with any industry participant".

Total independence from industry participants is not essential. On the contrary, the buy-in of key industry partners may be essential for success — so long as the exchange is not controlled by such parties and has a strong, independent advisory board (see Chapter 11).

Technology Partners

Since successful B2B Exchanges are fundamentally business solutions, the technology is something that can be outsourced or acquired through a strategic partnership.

e-STEEL is a good example of a successful strategic partnership with a technology expert — Computer Services Corporation (CSC). CSC has 49,000 employees in more than 700 offices worldwide in areas such as management and information technology consulting, systems consulting and integration, operations support, and information services outsourcing. CSC's revenues exceed $7.4 billion per year.

CSC provided the credibility on the technology side that enabled e-STEEL to quickly build a high level of trust with the main steel-producing companies whose "buy-in" was critical to the success of their on-line steel exchange.

Information Providers

Building value for members of an exchange requires the exchange to provide as many additional services around the central market space as it can. Rather than building lots of new services, it makes more sense to bring these services in through strategic partners for whom that service is their core competency. This is particularly true in the case of information services.

The classic success story in the information vending business is the meteoric rise of Michael Bloomberg's eponymous company. Bloomberg started by focusing on the bond trading business. He built up a database of historical pricing information on US bonds which is unrivalled to this day. Around this database he added strong analytic functions to which traders had not previously had instant access. Then he threw in real-time news updates. The Bloomberg box quickly became the only information device that a US bond dealer needed in order to follow the markets and keep up to date.

Successful B2B Exchanges will build into their systems access to tailored information feeds that ensure that a trader in their

vertical does not need any other information device in order to trade in that space.

To do this quickly, it makes sense to bring in the information rather than trying to compete with the hundreds of news wire and news syndication services. The Catex risk exchange turned to Hughes Data services for provision of detailed weather services on their site. MetalSite has formed a partnership with Reuters who supply customized "Metal Industry" news feeds.

Community Services

As we shall see in Chapter 13, a successful B2B Exchange must become a virtual community. To do this quickly, the exchange must add a number of value-added community services.

The fastest way to do this is to form strategic partnerships with one or more companies that specialize in the provision of such services.

The type of services required, and the potential partners, are as follows:

- customized news feeds (Reuters);
- documents "extranet" center (IntraLinks);
- supply chain management (Skyway);
- escrow services (i-escrow); and
- credit analysis (ecredit.com).

• • • • • • • • • • • • • •

Chapter Summary:

- *B2B exchanges must partner with key suppliers, commerce communities, and information providers to scale up quickly.*
- *A B2B Exchange needs to achieve "buy-in" from one or more of the 800-pound gorillas in its vertical in order to dominate that vertical and to gain sufficient credibility to persuade the others to follow.*
- *Industry involvement must be balanced, however, by a strong and independent advisory board.*
- *Potential partners include a technology expert (e.g. e-STEEL and CSC).*
- *Potential partners include information vendors to add real-time news and data services.*
- *Other partners are providers of additional value services which help to build an exchange community.*

Chapter 8:

Revenue Models

Off-line exchanges have established revenue models based largely on the structure of stock exchanges, but the B2B on-line space is creating new forms of revenue opportunities. At present, the types of revenue that can be generated by a B2B Exchange are:

Revenue Source	Stock Exchange Models	Internet B2B Exchanges
Transaction fees	✓	✓
% of cost savings	✗	✓
Posting fees	✗	✓
Subscription (or membership) fees	✓	✓
Listing (or hosting) fees	✓	✓
Information selling fees	✓	✓
Information licensing fees	✓	✓
Advertising and permission marketing fees	✗	✓
Revenue sharing	✗	✓
Software licensing fees	✓	✓

Transaction fees

Since exchanges provide a centralized market space it follows that if they are successful they can charge a fee for each trade made using the facilities of the exchange. The usual format is to charge a fee based on the value of the transaction, sometimes with a minimum per trade or a maximum per trade for large deals. On the other hand, transaction fees can discourage trading in the early stages.

Securities exchanges have always charged transaction fees based on the value of the trade. Catex charges a commission on insurance contracts that are concluded as a result of an introduction made in the "post and browse" at the rate of ten basis points, or one-tenth of 1%, of the cash value of each transaction. The cost of the commission is borne by the parties involved in the transaction in such proportions as they agree to. At e-STEEL there are no membership or application fees, but e-STEEL charges a transaction fee of 7/8 of 1% to sellers; buyers never pay fees on e-STEEL. Similarly, PaperExchange charges the seller a transaction fee of 3% of the value of the transaction for paper-related and equipment listings. The National Transportation Exchange charges a transaction fee based on the size of a load.

With financial services, the value of the security or swap may run into the hundreds of millions of dollars, but the arranging parties are only prepared to pay a very small percentage in transaction fees, or even just a fixed fee. This is due to the enormous amount of competition in that market space and one of the key issues in securing large mandates is to keep the transaction costs to an absolute minimum.

One issue for a post and browse exchange is how to ensure that the transaction fee is paid, given that members who meet through the Bulletin Board can easily go off-line to conclude the deal. One solution is for the exchange to ensure that it has a contract with each trading member whereby they are bound to report any deals closed as a result of a connection established through the system — and to rely on the integrity of members to report trades. This can be reinforced in the web site by requiring the parties to communicate through the exchange so that the exchange's administration staff can monitor their activities.

One way to make users communicate through a system in the early stages is to make the initial communications take the form of anonymous postings and responses. This means that the buyer and seller cannot find out who each other are until after they have exchanged communications within the B2B Exchange's system, thus enabling the deal to be tracked by the exchange.

For example, PaperExchange does not reveal the names of the buyer or the seller to either party until after they have concluded a trade through the exchange's anonymous bidding system. Similarly, on CreditTrade the parties to a trade must "lock" the trade in the system once they agree on the terms. The contractual agreement is then finalized off the system, but the parties must come back to the system to either "unlock" the trade, if it did not complete successfully, or confirm that it was executed.

In a relatively small user community this will usually work, as the exchange is likely to hear about trades eventually through industry sources. With an auction system or an electronic execution system the exchange has a full electronic audit trail regarding every trade on which to base the transaction fee invoices to members.

One strategic issue for an emerging B2B Exchange is whether to forego or reduce the transaction fee in the early stages in order to encourage users to trade through the exchange. Since liquidity is king in persuading industry players to change the way they currently do business and to join the exchange, it helps to be able to report significant deal flow through the exchange's facilities. Waiving or reducing the fee at the start for an introductory period thus helps to bring players onto the exchange and to encourage use of the central market space. Charging a transaction fee can also damage the exchange's relationship with key players at the start-up stage.

B2B Exchanges also have a unique opportunity to charge a buyer based on a percentage of the cost savings that result from the use of the exchange. However, such a fee can only be charged in the year in which the savings actually occur and will decline over time as the size of the savings decline.

Posting fee

In lieu of a transaction fee — or in addition to a transaction fee — an exchange can charge a fee for each "posting" or order entered into the system. Nasdaq, for example charges a fee for every quote that a market-maker puts into the Nasdaq system, in addition to a transaction fee on executed trades.

Again, there is a dilemma of whether to permit free postings initially in order to encourage volume or whether to charge. One solution to this dilemma is to charge a posting fee, but to provide volume discounts that move rapidly toward a zero cost if a player makes a lot of postings (thus adding to the value of the exchange). At PaperExchange for example, there are no fees for posting bids and offers.

Subscription (or membership) fees

When an exchange registers a new member it can charge a one-time joining fee and an annual maintenance fee for retaining the membership. This fee can be a lump sum payable in advance each year, or a monthly subscription fee for use of the system. Again, in many cases, B2B Exchanges waive this fee for a certain period to encourage early membership.

Internet-based exchanges can track this easily by implementing secure user name and password access to the trading screens and other "members only" parts of the web site. Clearly, it is attractive to new members if they can sign up for a free trial period or if they can access the site to view information — but not to post offers or respond to offers — for a reduced fee or for no charge. The CreditTrade web site permits you to register as a "visitor" for free, which provides you with access to various parts of the site, but not to the "Crown jewels" — the trade postings of potential deals. On the other hand, PaperExchange allows all visitors to see the live postings; however, a user name and password is necessary in order to respond or counter-bid. PaperExchange does not currently charge any joining fees.

Listing (or hosting) fees

Where an exchange permits users to list products on the system for trading on the exchange, it can charge those users a fee for "listing" the products on the exchange.

In the case of securities exchanges this has taken the form of a listing fee that is charged whenever an issuer has securities admitted to listing and trading on the exchange. It should be noted that, in this case, the exchange assumes a regulatory role in respect of securities that are listed on the exchange and establishes a direct contractual relationship with the issuer of the securities. For example, the exchange ensures that the issuer of the securities makes full disclosure to the market regarding any information which might affect the price of the securities, the volume of trading or the ability of the issuer to meet its financial commitments (what stock exchanges call price-sensitive information). Some stock exchanges will admit securities for trading on the exchange without listing those securities — in which event the exchange has no direct relationship with the issuer of the securities and does not profess to regulate that issuer. The Bermuda Stock Exchange, for example, allows trading members to print trades made in securities that are listed on the NYSE or Nasdaq even though those securities are not listed on the BSX.

For B2B Exchanges that trade physical products, this fee can take the form of a hosting charge to suppliers for them to set up their virtual storefront within the exchange's web site.

For example, VerticalNet charges a fee to host the supplier's storefront and list the supplier's products in its commerce-enabled web site. These hosting or listing fees currently comprise the majority of VerticalNet's revenue stream.

Information selling fees

Once an exchange has established the power of its central market, it has the economic power to charge users for valuable information that only the exchange has — for example, the trading information for each day and historical trading data.

Securities markets use information vendors to disseminate their information globally and charge those vendors for receiving the data feeds from the exchange. Reuters, Bloomberg and Bridge/Telerate are the largest information vendors and they all pay a fee to the larger stock exchanges in order to receive a real-time feed of trading and pricing data from the exchange. The information available from smaller exchanges is not as valuable to the information vendors so they generally will not pay a fee for it, but they are usually willing to carry the data on their systems (without paying for it) in order to be able to claim that their screens are the most comprehensive information sources.

Some B2B Exchanges take the view that the trade data is so valuable that they must restrict access to that data to paying subscribers only. In some markets the trade data available on deals made through the B2B Exchange will be unique information which was not previously available to players in that market space, and the exchange may wish to preserve the value of that information by restricting access to it. For example, Manheim Online charges a fee for car dealers to buy the list of all the sale prices from the on-line auctions held each day. Clearly the current fair market value of used cars sold through the web site is very valuable information to the dealers.

This approach limits the initial visibility of the exchange and can slow down the overall rate of take-up in the industry. On the Internet it is often sensible to give information away at the start in order to build your market share and develop relationships with users.

We believe that new B2B Exchanges should seek to provide the widest dissemination of their trade information, by making it freely available at the beginning, in order to build market awareness of their exchange. The Exchange can then look to charge a fee for the data if they develop to the point where their information is truly unique and valuable.

Information licensing fees

The pricing information that comes out of an active exchange can sometimes be used to create new products, such as futures or options contracts that are "derived" from the cash prices. Such derivative contracts can themselves be traded. In these circumstances, the exchange can charge a licensing fee for the use of the pricing data in the formulation of the derivative contracts.

In the securities world, the most obvious example of this is the Dow Jones and Standard & Poor's Indices in the US. In each case the index is based on the prices at which the constituent stocks trade on the NYSE or Nasdaq. Both S&P and Dow Jones charge large license fees to the Chicago Mercantile Exchange and the Chicago Board of Trade (respectively) for the use of those indices to trade derivative contracts. If the NYSE and the Nasdaq had formulated those indices, then those exchanges would be able to charge a license fee for the use of the data. In the United Kingdom, the London Stock Exchange (LSE) has a 50/50 joint venture with the *Financial Times* called FTSE International which creates and publishes the leading equity and bond indices in the UK and Europe. The FTSE 100 index is based on the pricing data published by the LSE.

Advertising and permission marketing fees

In the Internet Age, a B2B Exchange that establishes itself as a portal in a specific industry vertical will be able to charge fees for banner advertising and other extended listing services on its web site.

VerticalNet is a good example of a form of B2B Exchange that already derives a substantial part of its revenue from advertising, or sponsorships, carried on its web site.

Extended listings are similar to on-line Yellow Pages. The B2B Exchange provides a comprehensive directory of the key industry players or a collection of suppliers' storefronts and charges firms a premium price in order to enlarge or enhance their listing with graphics, hypertext links to their own web sites, etc.

Advertising on the Web is evolving rapidly. Many people have already realised that banner ads are not very effective on the Web and, in fact, have received a poor reception. The good news is that when it comes to Internet advertising, banners are not the only game in town. Opt-in e-mail marketing — sending commercial e-mail messages to targeted lists of Internet users who have opted-in to receive them — is generating click through rates as high as 20% and helping publishers, catalogers, and E-commerce companies to reach their target market quickly, cheaply and responsibly.

Customer retention and loyalty are two key themes that B2B Exchanges must use to differentiate themselves from the competition. All of the registered users of the exchange can be 'opt-in' recipients of information based on the specific areas of interest that they have indicated on sign-up. Members should therefore be offered the choice of 'opting-in' to certain targeted e-mail advertisements when they subscribe to the exchange — perhaps for a reduced subscription fee. In this way, the B2B exchange will be able to participate in the rapidly growing market for opt-in e-mail marketing — now called "permission marketing" by carefully selling access to its membership list.

Revenue sharing fees

B2B Exchanges can generate revenues through strategic partnerships with business partners who provide analytics, ratings, and news services, or the exchange can publish and sell its own data and analytics.

Stock exchanges have traditionally missed the opportunity to provide information and analytical services around the central market trading facility. This is because the stock exchanges have traditionally been owned by the brokerage firms who themselves make a lot of money from providing such information and analytical research to their investment clients. So, to avoid competing with their owners, stock exchanges have not generally used the information generated by their own exchange; instead they have allowed their broker members to use that data.

New B2B Exchanges that are structured as for-profit, open membership exchanges must take full advantage of the opportunities presented to generate revenue from advanced analytical research and data reporting services. Although the exchange cannot provide direct recommendations on the products available for trading on the exchange, the exchange can sell all of the raw data and analytical services that are required for buyers and sellers to make informed trading decisions.

Software licensing fees

If the exchange develops a sophisticated trading platform with integrated logistics and back-office functionality, it is possible to license this software to other exchanges in different verticals which are not directly competitive.

However, there are a number of software companies such as Tradex, Maoi Technologies, and Tradeum that are now specializing in producing trading system software for multiple B2B Exchanges. It therefore makes more sense to partner with one of these specialist suppliers, than to spend a lot of time developing software with a view to licensing it to other exchanges. Indeed, stock exchanges have traditionally developed their own internal systems at huge expense and then found that outside software specialists have been able to develop more efficient systems that get licensed to competing exchanges.

• • • • • • • • • • • • •

Chapter Summary:

- *Transaction fee model — new exchanges need to waive or provide discounts for volume trades in the early stages.*
- *Posting fee model — may discourage early usage of the site.*
- *Discounts may need to be given for volume of postings/ transactions in order to attract liquidity.*
- *Listing fees and product introduction fees include charging suppliers a fee to host their virtual storefronts at the exchange.*
- *Membership fees (initial and annual) — potential conflict between driving early membership and raising revenue.*
- *Sale of data and other services model — (e.g. stock exchanges sell price, volume and transaction data) — conflict between open access to information and raising revenue.*
- *We believe that new B2B exchanges should seek to provide the widest dissemination of their trade information, for free at the beginning, in order to build market awareness of their exchange. The Exchange can then look to charge a fee for the data if they develop to the point where their information is truly unique and valuable.*
- *Advertising (sponsorship) and permission marketing fees are unique to the Internet and can be a part of a B2B Exchange's revenue.*
- *B2B Exchanges should seek revenue sharing models with business partners like analytics, ratings, and news service providers.*
- *Software licensing fees — wonderful if you can get them, but exchanges should let specialist software companies develop and license the systems.*

Part III

Seven Secrets for Success for B2B Exchanges

Chapter 9:

Secret #1 Stay Focused — Specialize on a Vertical

The most important secret of success in the initial phases of developing a B2B Exchange is to target a specific industry in which you have strong expertise, and then **specialize on a vertical** within that industry.

Specialization enables you to dominate your chosen space quickly, which creates mind share and liquidity, and then helps you to scale up quickly. Specialization also enables you to tailor your business model to match the target market's distinct characteristics. These are critical success factors at the start.

Once you have dominated your chosen vertical you can start to widen the scope of the exchange into other verticals within your chosen industry, but you can only achieve this luxury if you have proven liquidity and you have demonstrated the ability to dominate.

An exchange's main value proposition is in bringing together and matching up buyers and sellers, it follows therefore that a successful exchange brings together buyers and sellers who are interested in buying or selling the same, or similar, products. In the physical world, a car auction is not followed by a cattle auction, because each of those markets has different players and each market requires different storage and delivery mechanisms. In the virtual world the differences between on-line markets may not be as pronounced, but they still exist and the players in each market are very different — hence the need to specialize at the start.

MetalSite (www.metalsite.net) is a good example of an exchange with a specific focus from the outset. Situated as a trading hub for the steel industry, this exchange started off by trading surplus or second-grade metals only. This unique specialization allowed it to dominate that vertical. They selected these products initially because the existing players were more willing to participate in a new market for those products, without feeling that their core businesses were being threatened. Having established a good name, some great publicity and a proven ability to trade sub-standard steel, MetalSite is now able to expand its product range and to introduce primary-grade steel as a product.

Not every exchange will be a winner in its chosen vertical space; only the sites with proven liquidity will succeed.

In the exchange business liquidity is king. Sellers will gravitate to the market that has the most buyers, and buyers like the market that has the best supply.

Once you start to dominate a particular market you can quickly build further market share because your proven liquidity attracts more suppliers and thus more buyers — in a virtuous spiral.

Vertical Portals

Industry sectors can be divided into "vertical" market spaces. Each industry may be divided by geography, regulations, or product characteristics. These divisions act like fissures in the on-line world and can allow different B2B Exchange markets to service each of the separate verticals.

A regulatory division is evident in the securities markets between securities which are registered with the US SEC and which can therefore be sold to the US public, and securities that are not registered in the US. The Bermuda Stock Exchange (www.bsx.com), which is not subject to regulation by the SEC, is able to develop as a unique stock exchange by specializing in these non-US registered securities, even though it is located less than 780 miles from the NYSE.

An example of product differentiation is the initial specialization of MetalSite in scrap metals rather than primary-grade steel. The industry is the same, the steel industry, but the product differentiation has enabled MetalSite to build a dominant position in those products.

In other words, a laser-like focus on a specific product category, or vertical within an industry, can still yield a profitable space for a unique B2B Exchange.

A good example of a market divided by geography is the market for electricity. Electricity is a difficult product because it has to be consumed quickly after it is generated (you cannot store megawatts of power on a warehouse shelf) and it cannot be transported too far from the generator. This means that power generated in the US cannot be exported to an overseas market, such as Europe.

As a result, the vertical spaces available for B2B Exchanges in the electricity market are divided by geographical location.

This has enabled a successful B2B electricity market to develop in Scandinavia (www.skm.se), at the same time as Elinex is developing as a separate — but related — B2B electricity exchange in the US. Where a product can be shipped around the world, the vertical market space for that product is global and the dominant B2B Exchange is likely to be a global market, unless there are regulatory barriers that prevent a truly global market from developing.

Another special type of market space is where a particular type of buyer or seller is sufficiently homogenous in their interests that they represent a unique "vertical", even though they may cut across several industries. For example, small business buyers can have identical interests in aggregating their orders for numerous different types of product in order to secure better prices. This is the market space that Shop2gether is pursuing. Similarly, the sellers of excess inventory and surplus goods are sufficiently homogenous across multiple industries to support a specific vertical focus. This is the space that Tradeout is targeting. Where a special market space cuts across multiple horizontal markets it can be described as a "diagonal".

Choose a Monster Market

Some of these B2B markets are enormous in terms of value. For example, the market for paper in the US is worth at least $650 billion (PaperExchange), the market for steel sold in the US is $600 billion (MetalSite and e-STEEL), the US market for plastics is $390 billion per annum and the worldwide market for wholesale re-insurance (excluding life products) is at least $100 billion in premiums (Catex).

Secondly, some markets are more active than others. For example the market for nuclear power stations is worth several billion dollars, but they are only bought and sold infrequently. Conversely, in the paper industry there are lots of trades each day.

It obviously makes more sense to focus on the monster markets where there is frequent trading and where the most profits will be made.

Vertical Knowledge

Experienced vertical industry professionals should develop B2B Exchanges. Preferably the founders should be working within their chosen industry, but have the vision to see that, with Internet technologies now being adopted by business, there is an enormous opportunity for them to leave their Industrial Age corporations and start up a B2B Exchange. These professionals have deep knowledge of their particular industry and strong relationships with the main buyers and sellers in that vertical space.

This vertical knowledge is critical for the exchange to build credibility within the vertical quickly and to ensure that the exchange is tailored to suit that particular market.

The vertical knowledge of the founders of an exchange can be a major barrier to entry for potential competitors. Accordingly, a B2B start-up Exchange should concentrate on the vertical in which the founders have the most industry experience, or in which they can most easily buy-in that expertise.

A Case Study: Effects of Globalization on Securities Markets

The recent success of ECNs in attracting market share away from the traditional stock exchanges is a timely warning for all traditional markets of the power of the Internet to globalize markets which were previously constrained by geography.

During the first half of the twentieth century, stock markets flourished in all of the free market developed economies. Local stock exchanges proliferated — there used to be 13 stock exchanges in the United Kingdom and there are still 21 regional stock exchanges in India for example. Local markets could exist because the securities were evidenced by physical stock certificates (which had to be physically delivered to the buyer to effect settlement), and because the companies traded on these regional exchanges were mainly small companies with a local flavor. As the trading world expanded and companies became first national and then international, their shares were traded on a more national and then international basis. This led to pressure on the local exchanges to merge into one national exchange in order to pool the liquidity in these securities. In 1976, for example, the London Stock Exchange absorbed the 13 regional exchanges into one national stock exchange. Now the growth of international investment flows is generating pressure to create "pan-global" exchanges.

The next major innovation was the development of central securities depositories (CSDs). A CSD immobilizes the physical certificates, which represent stocks and bonds, and creates instead book-entry records of ownership. The result is that share trades can be settled electronically without any transfer of physical paper. Now shares can be traded electronically in a continuous, auction market system (see Chapter 5) and then settled electronically. This enables massive volumes to be traded — for example, on a good day in New York in 1999 over one billion shares changed hands — and for investors' orders to be received from all over the world.

Today, the world's largest stock exchanges are in turmoil. The acceptance of the Internet as one global communications standard has enabled electronic trading systems, called ECNs in the US, to develop a global reach in less than three years; whereas it took the NYSE more than 200 years to build its global reach and brand name. Suddenly the anti-competitive restrictions and cost inefficiencies that have developed within the broker-owned and -controlled traditional stock markets are being cruelly exposed.

ECNs are for-profit and fully electronic, so they are driving down the cost of trading and are providing pricing efficiencies by using central limit order books to directly match buy and sell orders.

The only way forward for these older exchanges is to "de-mutualize" and become more competitive. This is evidenced by the headlong rush of the NYSE, Nasdaq, London and Toronto stock exchanges to announce proposals to turn themselves into for-profit, shareholder companies and to go public themselves. However, not all of the brokers who own these securities exchanges will agree to upset the status quo and reshape their profitable ways of doing business. For example, the members of the International Petroleum Exchange — a derivatives market based in London — recently rejected the management's proposals to de-mutualize.

The small traders and local members who own and control the world's largest derivatives markets in the world — the Chicago Board of Trade (CBOT) and the Chicago Mercantile Exchange (CME) — are facing the same "tsunami". Both exchanges have long defended their open out-cry pit trading mechanism, despite the enormous cost of bringing thousands of traders together in huge trading floors, and have restricted the voting power of the large institutional firms who provide the capital that supports their markets. Indeed, the very existence of two competing derivatives markets which are the size of the CBOT and CME, in the same city — each with its own clearing house and billion dollar trading floor — is a unique monument to some of the inefficiencies of the Industrial Age. **In the New Economy, the winner takes most, and successful B2B Exchanges will so effectively dominate their chosen vertical that two similar exchanges will not be able to co-exist for as long as the Board of Trade and the "Merc" (as they are affectionately called) have.**

On an electronic platform it is possible to trade all forms of securities side by side — including stocks, bonds and derivatives. This fact has undermined the previous physical separation of stock exchanges (the NYSE and Nasdaq) from commodities exchanges (the CBOT and CME). As a result, securities markets outside of the US have been rapidly consolidating the trading of shares and derivatives into one exchange. In Germany, the Deutsche Börse now operates both markets. In Amsterdam, the oldest stock exchange in the world and the EOE derivatives market have merged to form Amsterdam Exchanges, in Sweden the OM Gruppen now owns and operates the stock exchange and the derivatives market. In both Hong Kong and Singapore, the respective governments have mandated the merger of the stock exchange and the derivatives exchange.

The race is now on to create one global market space for all types of major financial securities, including shares, bonds, and derivatives — and in the end, there is likely to be only one big winner.

Nasdaq has recently merged with the American Stock Exchange (AMEX — which interestingly enough already trades options contracts and holds a license to run a futures market in the US) and has announced deals to link up with exchanges in Japan, Australia, Hong Kong and possibly the Deutsche Börse in Europe. Meanwhile, the Deutsche Börse, London Stock Exchange and six other European exchanges are working on the establishment of a "pan-European", electronic exchange for the top 300 securities in Europe.

However, this global market space will only exist for a small percentage of securities — that is, only those securities which can command worldwide liquidity and attention. This is why the proposed pan-European exchange is focusing on the top 300 securities only. There will still be a role for national stock exchanges, trading the securities of companies that do not have global appeal, acting as nurseries for small, high-growth companies that have the aspiration to one day be traded on the "**Global 1,000**" system. But, in future, purely national exchanges will have to face the dishonor of seeing their biggest and best stocks moving on to this pan-global market space.

We believe that, in the same way, other markets will be divided into global market spaces, smaller, purely national markets, and very small local markets.

We have analyzed this globalization effect in some detail because it will effect all businesses that operate outside of a purely local context. The securities markets have been impacted so rapidly and noticeably because they were already relatively efficient, and trade products that are now totally digital, fungible and fully "commoditized".

Over the next ten years, most physical markets will be impacted by the same dynamics and face the same global competitive pressures. They will all witness the walls of their ancient citadels shake and then crumble.

And the army blowing their trumpets loudest at the ramparts will be the B2B Exchanges that are now emerging.

The Rainforest Effect

In the ecosystem of a rainforest, there is intense competition to reach the sunlight. Covered by the dense canopy of the overhanging trees, many plants learn to live in the shadows and provide ground cover. Others thirst for greater glory and have to grow thin, tall, and fast in order to pierce through the existing canopy and break out into the sunlight above. Once those high achievers reach the light they can afford to spread out, develop branches and leaves and add to the lush green canopy. In the same way, B2B Exchanges must focus on a vertical, scale up quickly and grow as fast as they can. Once they break through the canopy and achieve dominance, mind share and credibility in that vertical, they can afford to spread out and introduce new products, attack other verticals, and add extra services.

For example, PaperExchange started off in the containerboard and fine paper segments. However, once it had dominated these product verticals, it incorporated all major grades of paper, including paperboard, newsprint, and scrap paper products. Now its web site includes listings of equipment and machinery for sale. Listings range from presses and corrugators to an entire mill.

PaperExchange's potential rivals are now facing the sunlight starvation of plants that are growing underneath the forest canopy.

• • • • • • • • • • • • •

Chapter Summary:

- *Target a specific industry — specialize on a vertical within that industry.*
- *Specialization helps you to scale up quickly and to dominate your space.*
- *Successful exchanges tailor their business model to match the target market's distinct characteristics.*
- *A market may be fissured by geography, regulations or product characteristics — select a vertical within an industry.*
- *An analysis of the effects of globalization on stock exchanges creates lessons for all markets in the next ten years — but global trading will only be relevant to a very small group of securities, leaving opportunities for smaller national exchanges.*
- *Once you have dominated one vertical, you can expand your product range based on your credibility and perceived expertise (the Rainforest Effect).*

Chapter 10:

Secret #2 Play to Win — the Need to Dominate

The benefits of specialization, which we describe in Chapter 9, mean that there will only be one major winner in each vertical sector. And that winner will take most in each vertical. This means that a successful exchange must try to be one of the **"first to market"** in its chosen vertical.

This powerful new paradigm derives from the fact that on the Network, success is self-reinforcing and is driven by the dynamics of increasing returns. Increasing returns will lead to a concentration of buyers and sellers in one B2B Exchange market space for each product. One B2B Exchange may operate several market spaces, but only one centralized market space is likely to dominate for each product.

In true Internet pioneering fashion, the founders of a new B2B Exchange must "plant their flag, declare victory, and then run like hell".

Viral Growth

In respect of B2B Exchanges the law of increasing returns means that the site with the most or the best buyers will attract the most or the best suppliers, which will generate transaction liquidity and that in turn will attract more buyers.

Liquidity attracts more liquidity in the exchange business.

The Virtuous Vortex

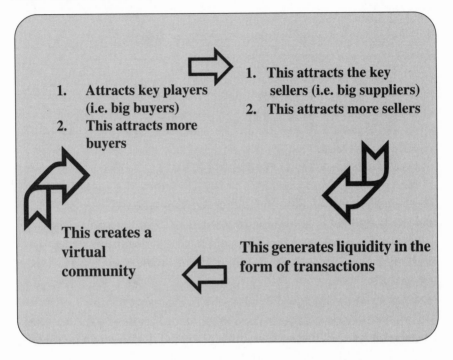

1. Attracts key players (i.e. big buyers)
2. This attracts more buyers

1. This attracts the key sellers (i.e. big suppliers)
2. This attracts more sellers

This creates a virtual community

This generates liquidity in the form of transactions

Once this virtuous circle has been set in motion, it acts like a vortex that sucks more players into the exchange and becomes self-sustaining in a sort of virtual perpetual motion.

In addition, this virtuous vortex creates a form of "positive polarity" that repels potential competitors. Since the successful exchange is generating the most liquidity and attracting the key players in that vertical market space, it becomes very difficult for a competitor to gain enough traction to start such a virtuous circle in its favor. One of the main reasons for this is that players who join one successful exchange will be reluctant to move to another exchange. A key player is unlikely to switch easily to another start-up exchange once it has:

- gone through the sign-up process with one exchange;
- got used to trading through that exchange; and

- if the exchange follows our formula for success with Secret 7, integrated its back-office systems and document processing with that exchange.

This means that a successful exchange which starts to dominate a vertical market space can create very high barriers to entry in that specific space.

Clearly, the first credible exchange to market has a significant advantage as it can establish its name and approach the key players before any other exchange. However, in the more traditional industries, being the first exchange may not always create an automatic winner, as it may take a long time to build up industry acceptance of this new form of business model. In such situations, the second or third mover may be able to learn from the mistakes of the first mover and benefit from the groundwork established by that first mover in selling the concept of an exchange mechanism. In addition, the second mover may be able to learn from the mistakes made by the early bird and, if that exchange has greater industry-specific experience (vertical knowledge) and greater credibility, the second mover can gain greater market acceptance and become the dominant player.

Liquidity, Liquidity, Liquidity

Achieving domination means having the greatest liquidity — that is, having the most trades done on your exchange. The main service an exchange provides is a centralized market space, and the more likely a buyer or seller is to make a satisfactory transaction on an exchange, the more likely they are to sign up and use that exchange over its rivals.

Liquidity is king for exchanges, so it is essential to build trading volume as quickly as possible.

Building the volume of trades is more important than numbers of members at the start. This means that you should target the key players who are likely to trade the most and get them to join early, rather than focusing on signing up the most number of members. In addition, if there are any intermediaries that can "make a market" they are like gold dust at the start. These key players help to create liquidity by smoothing out natural timing fluctuations in the number of buyers or sellers that are available at any particular point in time.

In the securities business, liquidity has *always* been king. Nasdaq succeeded as a market for smaller company stocks (which are naturally very illiquid) by providing two market-makers for each stock. These market-makers undertook to quote a bid and an ask price for their designated stocks on a continuous basis. The result being the investors can always trade in those stocks (albeit at the additional cost of paying the market-makers' "spread" — see Chapter 6). The success of the London Stock Exchange in the 1980s was built on the fact that it provided a more liquid market for trading many European stocks than the domestic market for those shares. For example, more Swedish companies' shares were trading in London than on the Stockholm Stock Exchange and about one-fifth of German shares were trading there rather than on the many regional exchanges in Germany. In fact, London became such a dominant market for trading European shares that the Exchange changed its name from the "London" to the "International Stock Exchange". This domination arose because London had a critical mass of large securities houses and many of them were prepared to make a market in these European securities from their dealing desks in London.

It is interesting to note that the way in which both the Stockholm and the Deutsche Börse have managed to re-engineer themselves and win back a dominant position in Swedish and German securities, respectively, has involved:

• abandoning the broker-owned model of ownership and closed membership through "de-mutualization" (see Chapter 5);
• turning themselves into profit-focused, commercial operations;
• adopting electronic trading systems which provide more efficient trading than London's market-maker system; and
• merging with rivals and with competing regional exchanges to create one dominant player.

The International Stock Exchange in London, on the other hand, failed to modernize during the early 1990s. Now it has lost its dominant position in most European securities and has changed its name back to the London Stock Exchange. Today, all the traditional stock exchanges in Europe face fresh competition from the new B2B Exchanges called ECNs such as POSIT, Tradepoint, Easdaq (which has just been restructured as a pan-European platform for low-cost securities trading), and a proposed new institutional crossing network called CrossNet.

Critical Mass

Liquidity is enhanced if you can build a critical mass of users as quickly as possible. This means that you must target the key players in your vertical, whether buyers or sellers, and make sure that they sign up with you. In order to achieve sign-up, most exchanges have to waive the standard subscription fees in the early stages. Waiving fees at the start can put a lot of pressure on an exchange's finances.

However, market share is worth more than profits in the early stages of the launch of a B2B Exchange.

In the B2C world, we have seen the development of a new valuation model, which is based on future revenue potential, not current net income, in order to capture the dynamics of the New Economy. The same dynamic of increasing returns applies to B2B Exchanges and this means that achieving domination in the early years can ensure future revenues in that vertical.

Signing up key players also creates a forward momentum that captures mind share as press releases and the standard "jungle telegraph" within each vertical pass on the word about the growth of an exchange. Conversely, low growth rates in the early stages can result in a serious loss of credibility. If an exchange creates a significant level of awareness at the launch and then does not deliver in terms of a credible level of transactions within a reasonably short time frame, then it will be harder to sign up more members.

This means that a successful exchange must organize a massive marketing and customer care program to win converts quickly. New users must be wooed, cajoled, and encouraged to sign up early and then smothered with good customer support in order to ensure that they use the exchange. This involves providing free training for each member's staff and constant contact with the member to make sure that user indifference does not prevent them from trading on your exchange in the early stages. For example, e-Chemicals places advertisements in chemical trade publications which focus on customer acquisition. The company's retention marketing efforts include follow-up communications via e-mail for new customers who have subscribed to the site, as well as direct mail pieces and auction invitations. e-Chemicals has a dedicated, direct sales force to sell its E-commerce procurement to large customers and suppliers, and targets small customers through telemarketing and direct marketing efforts.

One choice to make early on is whether to target buyers or sellers initially. An exchange must attract both buyers and sellers, but initially it is critical to attract a sufficient number of the party who will gain most from transacting over an exchange as opposed to their traditional transaction mechanisms. In the New Economy, this is likely to be the buyers, as they are usually empowered more by the introduction of Internet-based automation of the trading process. However, this is not always the case. For example, both PaperExchange and MetalSite have succeeded by targeting sellers first.

MetalSite initially secured commitments from major steel producers to commit inventory on a daily basis and to list a substantial volume of product for sale monthly. These steel suppliers were leaders and innovators in the national and international marketplace and brought both credibility and product to the MetalSite marketplace. Sometimes it takes market-makers to get a market going. For example, because electricity is not a commodity that "sticks around", it is important to have both buyers and sellers participating at the same time. To guarantee market liquidity and ensure that deals could be closed, Elinex initially targeted market-makers and special deals were negotiated with those who were willing to continually offer buy and sell price quotes.

Once a winner has critical mass there are very high barriers to entry for other potential exchange competitors, since inertia prevents members shifting from one exchange to another.

Domination vs. Anti-dilution

To achieve market domination in a chosen vertical when building a B2B Exchange, look to merge with competitors to gain a dominant position as quickly as possible. e-STEEL is some six months behind MetalSite in the steel industry vertical. In the huge chemicals market there are now several competitors, including Chemdex, SqiQuest, e-chemicals, Chemconnect, and others. In this type of scenario, one exchange is likely to gain a dominant position and then suck the oxygen out of the others. For the exchanges that find they are running in second or third place there is no point in worrying about trying to maintain market share against each other; they must merge and seek domination.

Winning as a B2B Exchange is about dominating your vertical; it is not about coming second or third while trying to avoid dilution of your existing market share.

For example, in September 1999, PaperExchange, the leading Internet trading marketplace worldwide for the pulp and paper industry, announced the acquisition of MPX, Inc., the developer of Mpexchange, an Internet-based, third-party exchange for the buying and selling of white paper grades. The acquisition expanded PaperExchange.com's already existing strong user base and strengthened the exchange's domination in printing and writing grades. For the founders of Mpexchange, the chance to join with PaperExchange and to dominate the market was far more attractive than competing with them for market share.

Cash Cappel, CEO of MPX, Inc., is quoted in the company's September 1999 press release as stating, "*We had been moving aggressively towards the launch of Mpexchange later this month; however, the opportunity to join forces with PaperExchange.com, the pioneer and by far the strongest on-line paper-based trading environment, was an incredible opportunity and too compelling to pass up. We are delighted to join forces with the very talented and focused PaperExchange team and contribute to increasing their market dominance.*"

On the other hand, don't forget that industries can be fragmented along many lines, such as geographical, regulatory, or by product category. This means that several exchanges may co-exist in the same industry.

Having complementary exchanges in the same industry can actually help to build an exchange by increasing awareness and acceptance of exchanges within that industry at the early stage. Subsequent mergers can ensure that an exchange dominates the whole industry sector.

Branding

Building a strong brand name is very helpful in achieving domination. The NYSE brand is powerful in the securities industry in the US and abroad, and Nasdaq struggles to compete with the pull of the "Big Board". In the paper industry, PaperExchange has already established a dominant brand, and in the transportation business in the US, the National Transportation Exchange already has strong branding.

One element of branding is the choice of name. In many cases this will be driven by what Internet domain names are still available — since a short, catchy URL is very helpful. One danger in choosing a name, though, is being too product-specific at the start. Initially, this may help in building brand recognition within your chosen vertical, but later it can become constraining as you expand the exchange into other complementary verticals and outgrow the name. For example, PaperExchange and e-STEEL are both very product-specific. The alternative is to choose a more general name, such as MetalSite (which allows them to expand from steel into other metals), or to adopt a catchy, non-product-specific name like Shop2gether.

The Catastrophe Risk Exchange has established a strong brand name for "Catex" in the insurance industry. Initially their focus was on trading large value property catastrophe risk contracts (known as "cat" contracts in the business). However, the name Catex could now be seen as a hindrance as it requires the exchange to constantly explain that they are NOT limited to just catastrophic risk products. CEO Frank Fortunato is quoted in an *Insurance Networking* article as saying that "a common misconception is that Catex focuses solely on catastrophe exposures….but Catex actually facilitates various risks, including environmental liability, marine, aviation, auto insurance and others; less than 50% of transactions involve catastrophe exposures". On the other hand, the name Catex is now widely recognized in the industry and a change would require a significant re-branding.

The same problem has been highlighted in the B2C world where companies such as eToys and Software.net have found that the name may not suit the company anymore as it grows. In the case of Software.net, the company expanded from just software into game cartridges and some hardware products, so it decided to change its name to "Beyond.com". On the other hand a generic name like "Amazon.com" can continue to work even when the company has expanded from book selling to on-line auctions, music sales, and others. Clearly it helps if you can get the right name at the start.

Always bear in mind that the correct name is not the only factor in determining success or failure; providing the best customer care and support is much more important in building brand recognition and trust amongst users.

Customer Care and Support

A successful B2B Exchange will spend the majority of its resources on building a strong customer care and support program in the early stages. Sometimes it is justified to spend up to 80% of your resources on obtaining new members and keeping the existing members happy.

Firstly, the exchange must focus on its potential customers with targeted marketing campaigns, both direct mail and one-on-one presentations and demonstrations. Potential trading members are particularly essential in the early stages in order to build liquidity on the exchange.

Secondly, in addition to the usual marketing efforts to secure new members, a B2B Exchange must have a thorough customer care and user support program for those users that sign up, which includes at least:

- regular training sessions that are free for members' staff;
- 24-hour, seven-days-a-week help desk — part or all of which can be outsourced;
- trading desk support function and trade facilitators to encourage new listings and trades — these staff must call the members regularly and make sure that the member is using the system to its full advantage and encourage them to use it more;
- an organized system of receiving feedback from trading members; and
- dispute resolution mechanisms.

Prepare for the Long Haul

Achieving domination will not happen overnight. Indeed, if an exchange represents a paradigm shift for the industry, then you must be prepared for a long haul in getting "buy-in" and wide usage. Catex took two years of constant sales tours to persuade the traditionally conservative insurance industry that risk could be traded on a computer screen.

In our experience, the firm resistance to change that start-up B2B Exchanges encountered some two years ago has now become a nervous acceptance within most companies that they must embrace the Internet and accept the changes it is bringing.

Many industries will argue that their business depends on personal contacts and face-time. This process facilitates the development of intermediaries who can charge large commissions for bringing potential business partners together. In fact, no industry is unsuitable for automation of the transaction process through an on-line B2B Exchange — but some industries will resist the process more than others. In every case though, human interaction in signing-up new members and in encouraging them to use the new exchange's system will still be very important in the early stages of growth.

• • • • • • • • • • • • •

Chapter Summary:

- *Specialization means that there will only be one major winner in each vertical sector.*
- *The winner will take most in each vertical.*
- *Try to be one of the first to market in your vertical — "plant your flag, declare victory, and then run like hell".*
- *If you are not dominating your market, look to merge with competitors — winning as a B2B Exchange is about domination; it is not about coming second or third by avoiding dilution of your market share.*
- *Liquidity is king for exchanges so build volume of trades as quickly as possible (for example, liquid stock exchanges always attract business from competitors).*
- *Build a critical mass of users as quickly as possible — slow growth rates result in a loss of credibility.*
- *You need a massive marketing and customer care program to win converts quickly.*
- *Market share is worth more than profits in the early stages (for example, B2C valuation models based on future revenue potential, not current net income).*
- *Once a winner has critical mass, there are very high barriers to entry for other exchange competitors.*
- *Building a great brand name is very helpful (NYSE is the "Big Board" and Nasdaq has to compete with that image) — but there is a danger in having a name which is too restrictive.*
- *Don't fear other exchanges in the same industry if they are constrained from competing directly with you by regional geography or product characteristics.*
- *If your exchange represents a paradigm shift for the industry then be prepared for a long haul in getting "buy-in" and wide usage.*

Chapter 11:

Secret #3 Maintain Commercial Neutrality

Because an exchange provides a centralized market space for multiple competing members, and both buyers and sellers, it must stay neutral in order to be credible and build trust.

The need for neutrality must permeate the whole exchange, the way it is designed, the way it operates, and the way in which it secures users' confidential information. The exchange's trading rules must not favor any single participant.

This means that the exchange must be perceived as a neutral third party by all other parties, as well as actually acting as a neutral body and it must be designed to benefit all the players in the industry that it serves.

The reason why B2B Exchanges are being developed primarily by individuals who have worked within an industry, but are now leaving their Industrial Age corporations to start up a B2B Exchange, is because their former corporate employer would find this almost impossible to do because of this neutrality issue. An exchange that is owned or controlled by one particular player, or one particular class of user, will not be perceived as being independent.

Stay Independent

Accordingly, it will be difficult to succeed if you are owned or controlled by just one user group, whether that is the buyers, the sellers, or the broker intermediaries in your chosen industry. Successful B2B Exchanges must avoid becoming owned or controlled by one group of users or one company. This may not be easy because as the exchange starts to succeed and grow, key strategic partners or specific user groups will seek to control you.

For example, several major steel mills took an equity interest in MetalSite at an early stage in order to ensure that their interests were represented in the development of the exchange. In March 1999, Chemdex announced that VWR, a large distributor of laboratory equipment, chemicals and supplies to the scientific marketplace, had acquired a 10% interest in Chemdex.

Where the exchange accepts investment by industry players, it must ensure that they do not achieve a control position and that their input is channelled through an independent process that ensures that all users' views are represented. We recommend that the exchange set up an independent advisory board that can help to counteract the purely commercial interests of that user group.

For example, when E W Blanche, a leading insurance broker, made an investment in Catex, the risk exchange went out of its way to ensure that it remained independent. In the press announcement regarding the investment, Catex stated that it had set up an independent board of governors to "oversee all functions of the exchange relating to neutrality and fair dealing".

In particular, a B2B Exchange should avoid allowing the members to gain control, as they can then restrict innovation in order to protect their existing businesses. As we saw in Chapter 5, the world's largest stock exchanges have traditionally been owned and controlled by the broker members (for example, the NYSE, Nasdaq and the London Stock Exchange). In many cases, this has restricted the ability of the exchange to introduce more efficient trading mechanisms, such as a central limit order book with automated execution. As a direct result, these exchanges now face increasing competition from ECNs and other trading systems that are sucking liquidity from the traditional stock exchange. The response of the management in each of these organizations, the world's three largest stock exchanges, has been to call for "de-mutualization" so that the exchange can be turned into a neutral, for-profit company with a wide ownership structure and the flexibility to innovate and change its business model.

The lesson for B2B Exchanges is to make sure you set yourself up as an independent, neutral party from day one.

Proportional Representation?

As a successful B2B Exchange develops and starts to dominate a particular industry, it will become increasingly important for that exchange to represent all of the users of that market space. One way to achieve this is to partition the ownership between different user groups. For example, the exchange could reserve part of its shares for buyers, part for sellers, part for intermediaries and part for the general public. In this way, it can be sure that all of the main user groups are properly represented in ownership and on the board of the company.

One danger of this approach is the temptation to develop proportional representation, whereby some user groups have greater voting rights. This arises because the largest user group will argue that it should have the most say in how the exchange is run. In order to keep that user group in the exchange, the founders may agree to give them greater voting rights. However, in the long run, this is a recipe for disaster.

The only fair form of corporate governance is a "one share, one vote" system. In such a system, a particular shareholder's influence is directly proportional to the amount of capital that they have provided.

Certain governance issues raise regulatory concerns, and these issues should be in the hands of an advisory board (see below).

The Chicago Board of Trade is a good example of how proportional representation can create a strait-jacket for the exchange as the market grows. At its inception, the CBOT traded only agricultural futures contracts — such as wheat, corn, and soybeans. Originally, the

135

liquidity in the CBOT's small commodity market came from the locals, (that is, individual traders who were prepared to speculate on the price of such physical commodities). In 1975, the CBOT expanded to include financial contracts, including US Treasury bond futures. As the derivatives markets grew, the financial products became the most popular and the world's largest banks, securities houses, and trading companies started to use such financial derivatives to hedge their risks or to make profits by speculating. Because the locals controlled the CBOT, the locals only agreed to admit the big investment banks, to trade the financial derivatives *if* the locals retained the voting control. So they created a proportional representation system whereby the locals are full members and have one full vote each, but the firms that just want to trade the financial products are only admitted as associate members and have only one-sixth of one vote each. Since there are in excess of 1,400 full members and less than 900 associate members, the locals can effectively outvote the corporate members.

In today's global economy, financial derivatives are a critical part of the financial system and the US Treasury bond future is the most actively-traded contract in the world. However, the firms that provide most of the capital to support that trading do not have equal voting rights at the CBOT because of the historical legacy of the control exercised by the locals. In fact, the largest corporate dealers are so upset with the failure of the CBOT to innovate in the area of electronic trading and to merge their clearing house with the Chicago Mercantile Exchange, that they have recently announced an intention to explore the potential of establishing a completely new, fully-electronic derivatives exchange in the US. This clearly demonstrates how a proportional voting system that may make sense at one point in time is unlikely to remain a good idea as the exchange grows and expands its product base.

Having the Flexibility to "Morph" the Business Plan

The B2B market space and the role of B2B Exchanges within that space is a dynamic environment. Although we have tried to provide some structure to the dynamics of this market space in this book, the world of business is now changing at Internet speed. This is why the cliché about the Internet heralding a revolution to rival or surpass the Industrial Revolution is actually quite true. The result is that B2B Exchanges must be incredibly light on their feet and able to innovate quickly.

Another cliché of the New Economy is that your business plan should be "morphed" (that is, re-written) every few months if you plan to stay ahead. That kind of flexibility is only possible in a highly entrepreneurial company which is not owned or controlled by Industrial Age structures.

Consider the dilemma faced by the management of Nasdaq. As we have seen elsewhere in this book, Nasdaq succeeded by providing a market-making system to create liquidity in small company stocks. This made it an attractive market space for high-growth technology stocks and many of those start-ups, like Microsoft and Dell, went on to become hugely profitable companies. As they grew and became successful, the shares of these companies became extremely liquid in their own right and Nasdaq began to rival the NYSE for liquidity and volume traded. This encouraged the successful companies to stay listed on Nasdaq rather than move their listings to the "Big Board" of the NYSE, which had previously been the mark of ultimate success for a public company.

However, Nasdaq failed to re-engineer the trading process for these types of stocks. Despite management attempts to introduce more efficient trading mechanisms, the members insisted on preserving the market-maker system, even though these types of stock are sufficiently liquid on their own. Because Nasdaq is owned and controlled by the market-making members the owners were able to resist any significant innovation or "morphing" of the business plan. The market-making system is very profitable in liquid stocks because the market-maker is able to keep the "bid-ask spread" (that is, the difference between the price that he buys at and the price that he sells at). This spread exists even though he is not taking much market risk because there are always lots of buyers and sellers (hence the natural liquidity). In addition, some market-makers colluded together to keep the "bid-ask spread" as wide as possible, which ultimately resulted in regulatory action by the SEC.

The result has been that more efficient competitors, starting with Instinet and now joined by nine other registered ECNs, have taken over 25% of Nasdaq's daily volume in the last two years. These ECNs are still pushing the envelope with the introduction of longer trading hours, international accounts for non-US investors, etc. Now Nasdaq is being forced to react to these competitive pressures and is looking to introduce a central limit order book, longer trading hours and international alliances to create a pan-global market space.

Maintain Confidentiality of Users' Data

Successful B2B Exchanges will build up an extremely valuable database of information about their chosen vertical market space. This data will include current prices, volumes and trades but also historical prices and volumes (for example, how much was this product trading for last year?) and product descriptions and details. Over time, this data will become a major component of the exchange's value proposition.

However, determining who has access to the data is a significant issue for each exchange.

Part of the confidential information that the exchange will build up includes sellers' product data and pricing, buyers' purchase history and price tolerance and the financial records of members. All of this data must be secured in a way that ensures a member's competitors cannot see that information and requires the exchange to have sound systems.

It may be necessary to have an independent auditor review the systems and business practices of the exchange on a regular basis in order to provide potential members with an independent confirmation that their data will be kept securely. For example, MetalSite provides an Arthur Andersen LLP independent report on the application of its core Business Principles, one of which is *"Information Protection and Privacy: MetalSite maintains effective controls to provide assurance that individual buyer and seller information is treated in a highly confidential and secure manner"*.

The Advisory Board and User Committees

As an independent third party which is providing a centralized market space that is tailored to the needs of a specific vertical market, a B2B Exchange must ensure that all of its user groups are represented in the decision-making process.

The easiest way to achieve this, without a complicated ownership structure or weighted voting, is to institute an advisory board and to set up committees comprising the different user groups.

The advisory board should be comprised of the highest-level industry representatives and highly credible thought leaders. The advisory board acts as a counterweight to the purely commercial interests of the shareholders and helps the exchange to be, and *appear* to be, a credible, neutral, and impartial marketplace. Within the exchange there should be a separate compliance function which reports directly to the advisory board.

The advisory board should provide a forum for the key players in the industry to have adequate input on policy without them having to have a controlling ownership interest or to control the board of directors.

In addition, user groups are a perfect way for different users to have input.

One user group that all B2B exchanges should have is an executive management committee. This committee should be legally structured as a sub-committee of the board and should have certain powers delegated to it by the formal board of directors so that it can meet regularly and oversee the day-to-day operations of the whole exchange. This committee can have representatives from the management of key players in all the main users groups of the exchange. However, the firms who they represent do not necessarily have to have any ownership or formal board representation in the company.

Another committee that all B2B Exchanges must have is a systems user group to ensure that management is always receiving feedback on the web site and other IT systems of the exchange from the actual users of those systems. Another common user group is the trading and settlement committee which should have representatives of the buyers, sellers and intermediaries, and which should approve the trading and settlement rules and regulations of the exchange.

An ideal committee structure for a B2B Exchange, based on our experience of running the BSX, is as follows:

Committee Structure

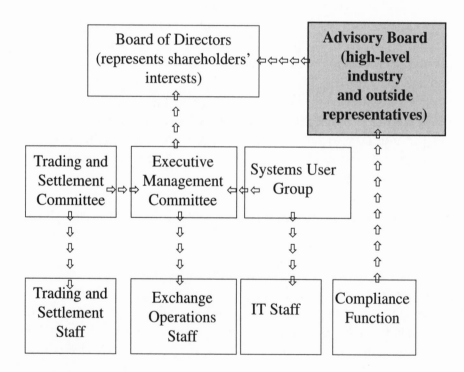

• • • • • • • • • • • • •

Chapter Summary:

• Exchanges need to stay neutral in order to be credible and build trust.
• An exchange must be seen to be impartial.
• Avoid becoming owned or controlled by one group of users or one company — as you grow, strategic partners or specific user groups seek to control you.
• Avoid members gaining control, as they then restrict innovation in order to protect their existing businesses (e.g. NYSE and other stock exchanges).
• Need to be able to continue to innovate, turn on a dime — business plan must be fluid.
• Users' confidential information must be protected and not available to competitors.
• Need for all user groups to be represented in decision-making — use of advisory boards and user committees.
• The advisory board should provide a forum for the key players in the industry to have adequate input on policy without them having to have a controlling ownership interest or to control the board of directors. A compliance function within the exchange should report directly to the advisory board.

Chapter 12:

Secret #4 Ensure Transparency and Integrity

Because an exchange provides a centralized market space for multiple competing members it must be an open and fair market in order to be credible and gain the users' trust. A fair market is one that is transparent and built on integrity.

Some members may resist this if they believe that they can profit more from inefficiencies in the market (for example, a lack of pricing transparency). Successful exchanges will set and enforce market rules that do not favor any one user or group of users.

A good example of this principle is MetalSite, which clearly states on its web site (www.metalsite.net) as follows:

"MetalSite is the premier electronic metals community where all interested parties can exchange information and goods through secure public and private channels. MetalSite's organization, policies and practices are structured to provide buyers and sellers of all types an unbiased and fair environment in which to conduct their day-to-day business.

MetalSite is a neutral market space for the exchange of goods and information among metal industry participants. MetalSite has created "Selling and Auction Rules" and a detailed "Privacy Policy" to communicate to our associates the guidelines and criteria by which our operations are conducted."

Need to be a Self-regulatory Organization

The exchange can only ensure it is open and fair if it is prepared to regulate the users of the exchange's centralized market facility. The form of regulation most appropriate for an Internet-based exchange is self-regulation. A B2B Exchange should be a self-regulatory organization (SRO); an SRO imposes regulations on its own members and then enforces those regulations.

Self-regulation is really enlightened self-interest, since it is always in the best interests of the exchange to maintain an open and fair market place.

Self-regulation should be contrasted with the alternative forms of regulation, which include regulation by an industry-wide association or regulation by a governmental body. Neither trade associations nor governmental bodies are sufficiently flexible to cope with the rapid development of the B2B market space; B2B Exchanges should thus ensure that they keep their own house in order so as to avoid calls for outside regulation.

Transparency

Transparency is a critical element of fairness and should be enforced by the exchange. At a minimum, all transactions made on the exchange should be reported promptly to the exchange with full details on price and volumes. With fully-automated execution, these details are immediately captured by the exchange's systems, but with post and browse and some auction-based exchanges the information must be given to the exchange by the parties to the trade.

The exchange should have rules and regulations that encourage transparency.

Different B2B Exchanges will offer different degrees of transparency depending on the balance they seek to strike between transparency and liquidity. For example, the London Stock Exchange allows market-makers to delay disclosing large trades to the market to encourage them to provide liquidity in the market and to avoid the adverse price movements that could result from the immediate disclosure of their largest trading positions. On the other hand, most ECN-type trading systems provide immediate (but anonymous) disclosure of every trade.

Pricing transparency creates a more efficient market, which often leads to lower prices. For example, in the reinsurance industry it is currently common for a large reinsurer to be dependent on an insurance broker to introduce business. This means that the broker controls the information about who is buying reinsurance and at what price. Since the industry is dominated by around four large brokers, those brokers control the flow of pricing information and the clients of one broker may not know what the clients of another broker are paying for the same product. The introduction of Catex is leading to screen-based trading of risks and enabling buyers and sellers of risk to meet each other through a neutral B2B Exchange. The premium price paid (called the "rate on line") for all trades made on Catex is posted onto the web site at www.catex.com. For the first time there is a degree of pricing transparency in the reinsurance market.

Full disclosure is the "mantra" of a fair and open exchange.

Transparency also applies to the products traded through the exchange's systems. Sellers must disclose full information about the items that they are selling so as to enable the buyers to make a reasoned assessment of the true value of the products. The exchange should therefore enable sellers to put full product specifications and details on the web site. Buyers will not return to a market where they purchase a "pig in a poke".

Integrity

The centralized pricing system is the most important function of an exchange, and the exchange must seek to ensure the integrity of that pricing mechanism. The key elements of a fair system are:

- equal access;
- the order with best price has highest priority;
- first in, first out (FIFO);

- effective procedures to ensure that each seller's products are posted correctly and that buyer bids and orders are transmitted accurately; and
- trades are consistently executed in accordance with the published rules of the exchange.

Equal access means that every trading member has equal access to the exchange's trading system, irrespective of size or duration of membership. Price priority means that any new order, which offers a better price, takes priority over existing orders. (That is, the lowest ask or the highest bid price must take priority over other orders with a less attractive price.) FIFO means that at the same price the time of entry of an order sets the priority of that order, with the first order received by the exchange taking priority over subsequent orders received at that price. With a fully electronic, auto-matching system, these rules can be hard coded into the system software using sophisticated algorithms.

To the extent that the exchange's trading rules cannot be "hard-wired" into the trading system, the exchange must introduce and enforce the trading rules against the members.

The rules of a successful B2B Exchange will require members to honor the integrity of the exchange's pricing mechanism. This means that members must agree not to do anything that will hinder or disrupt the fair and orderly functioning of the market. This should include a requirement that traders will not seek to manipulate the market, either on their own or through collusion with other members (for example, by spreading false information, misleading others about the true position of the market, or creating false trades to give the appearance of activity). All of these practices have a long and infamous history in the world of securities trading, and stock exchanges around the world have formed trade associations that issue standards of best practice and core principles for exchanges to implement in order to restrict them.

Finally, members should be under a general obligation not to mislead or deceive customers in advertising goods or services through the exchange or completing transactions through the exchange's systems.

The Exchange's Gatekeeper Role

In order to maintain credibility and trust, an exchange must regulate access to its centralized market space. In implementing this concept, the exchange must decide what standards and qualifications it will impose for joining the exchange and for continued membership. In all cases, the firm and the relevant employees of the firm should be fit and proper persons without any record of dishonest or fraudulent trading activities.

In a post and browse model, the exchange is providing a form of members' room where buyers and sellers can meet. In order to make such a mechanism effective and to ensure the integrity of the system, the exchange must pre-qualify entrants to the members' room. At least the exchange must ensure that they are legally able to buy or sell in that market and that they have some interest in buying or selling what is on offer on that exchange. In an auction-based exchange, the exchange must also ensure that the sellers are acceptable to the buyer for a reverse auction, (for example, in respect of the quality of their products and credit-worthiness), or that the buyers are acceptable to the seller for a normal auction.

In an auto-matching environment, the exchange must seek to ensure that buyers and sellers who are anonymously matched in the system can conclude the trade — otherwise, too many failed trades will destroy the credibility and integrity of the exchange. This may require the exchange to impose financial responsibility rules on members (for example, requiring members to have a minimum level of paid-up capital, or a minimum level of liquid assets or a minimum level of credit rating from an independent third party). Members must then be required to monitor and calculate their financial position with sufficient regularity to ensure that they remain in compliance with the exchange's minimum capital requirements.

There may also be wider regulatory issues to consider, particularly if the exchange trades products which are securities or commodities contracts. For example, CreditTrade enforces strict controls on who can access the trading portion of its site. In the United Kingdom the Financial Services Authority regulates the activities on the CreditTrade site and has not only established certain minimum standards of eligibility for trader access, but also requires regular reporting.

Cornering the Market

The exchange must seek to prevent the market from being dominated or cornered by any one user group.

One of the most infamous attempts to corner a market involved the Hunt brothers of Texas in 1979/80. In 1979, two Texas oilmen started amassing silver, much of it with borrowed money, in an attempt to corner the market. And they did corner it for a while; driving the price from $10 an ounce in 1979 to a high of $52 an ounce in January of the following year. At that price, people flooded the market with an excess of silver. When the price dropped, the Hunts' loans were called and they had to sell. On 27 March 1980 — later dubbed *Silver Thursday* — the Hunt brothers' attempt to corner the silver market finally ended. The price of silver plunged to $10.80 an ounce from $21.62 an ounce the day before, a 50% single day decline. This incident alone is often cited as justification for the heavy regulation of the commodities markets in the US that now exists under the Commodities Exchange Act.

This means that you should avoid setting up a B2B Exchange for markets that are dominated by a small number of suppliers or by one big buyer that can dictate the price. For example, the market for semiconductors is dominated by a small number of suppliers like Intel and is not suitable for a B2B Exchange.

Standardization

One of the value propositions of an exchange as opposed to an unregulated telephone market, lies in the standardization of the product, of the legal environment, of the trading and settlement terms, and of the documentation.

A successful B2B Exchange will draw up rules (or encourage members to adopt existing industry standards) that regulate the quality of the products offered on the exchange, the lot sizes in which they are offered, the way in which they are priced, the acceptable pricing increments (called the tick size), and the standard terms for trading and settlement. Many of these may be varied by agreement between the parties, but in the absence of specific terms, every trading member of the exchange should know that the standard terms set by the exchange will apply.

Regulating the quality of the products offered on the exchange helps to build trust in the exchange's centralized market space. Similarly, creating standardized documents and a common legal environment helps to avoid disputes and to build credibility in the integrity of the exchange.

Complaints and Dispute Resolution

The members of the exchange, as members of a community, should be required to honor the just and equitable principles of conduct set out in the exchange's rules and commonly practised in the market space where they are conducting business. This should include a requirement to honor the trading obligations to one another that arise from trading on the exchange.

Successful B2B Exchanges will provide a mechanism, which may be formal or informal, for a prompt and orderly resolution of complaints and disputes between trading members.

As B2B Exchanges are Internet businesses it makes most sense for the dispute resolution process to be an arbitration forum, set up in accordance with the International Arbitration standards and accessible on-line (that is, with documents being filed and arguments presented on-line).

Systems Integrity

The exchange must ensure that all of its systems are robust, so as to avoid systemic failures. As users become dependent on the exchange for pricing, trading and data it becomes more and more essential to provide fully redundant, highly secure systems. In the B2C space, the bad publicity experienced by eBay following several well-publicized outages of its core systems demonstrates graphically the dangers of system failures for a B2B Exchange.

Security of data on the exchange's systems must be high (for example, through the use of serious levels of encryption) to build up the trust of members. Members must be satisfied that their confidential data is secure within the exchange and that there can be no unauthorized use of that information.

Potential Regulation of Exchanges by Governments

Where a B2B Exchange becomes dominant in a marketplace it may raise public pressure to regulate the operations of that marketplace. For example, as PaperExchange becomes dominant as the price-setting mechanism for paper products worldwide, then the prices determined on PaperExchange will affect every business and every household product that uses paper (for example, the daily newspaper). This could lead to the belief that such an important B2B exchange should be required to operate for the public good, rather than purely as a private-sector, for-profit initiative.

This national interest ingredient may encourage the belief that some B2B exchanges should operate as "quasi-public utilities" rather than purely as private-sector, "for-profit" initiatives.

The securities markets are a classic example of such calls for regulation. The introduction of regulation of stock markets in the US came shortly after the 1929 Crash. Before the Crash, stock prices rose swiftly and steadily thanks to a post-World War I boom and to new and growing industries such as aviation, radio, and motion pictures. For the first time, the general public took a keen interest in trading. To become involved, however, many small investors had to borrow money. When the price of stocks plummeted in 1929, they went bankrupt trying to repay loans. Many companies, too, went out of business from lack of capital.

In the early 1930s, the US Congress sought to stabilize and regulate the securities marketplace by enacting two new laws: the Securities Act of 1933 and the Securities Act of 1934. The Securities Act of

1933 requires that securities offered through interstate commerce or the postal system must be registered with the federal government prior to public sale. It also requires that relevant financial information about the issuing company must be made available to potential investors through a document called a prospectus. The Securities Act of 1934 created the Securities and Exchange Commission and provided additional protective measures, such as prohibiting misrepresentation, manipulation and other abusive activities. The SEC's primary responsibility was — and still is — to administer the 1933 and 1934 Acts. The 1934 Act also provides that any company which operates a national stock market in the US must be registered as such with the SEC.

B2B Exchanges must adopt sound self-regulatory practices in order to avoid calls for legislation to regulate and license their activities as national markets once they become dominant in their industry.

• • • • • • • • • • • • •

Chapter Summary:

- *B2B Exchanges need to maintain an open and fair market in order to build credibility.*
- *There is a critical need for transparency in pricing and the product — this creates efficiencies and leads to lower prices. Some user groups may resist this.*
- *B2B Exchanges need to maintain the integrity of the pricing mechanism.*
- *B2B Exchanges need to regulate members' activities — and adopt a pre-qualified members' only room approach.*
- *B2B Exchanges must prevent the market from being dominated or cornered by any one user group.*
- *B2B Exchanges need to regulate product standards in order to build trust in the market.*
- *B2B Exchanges need to create or encourage the use of existing standardized contract terms to ensure integrity and avoid disputes.*
- *B2B Exchanges must ensure that their systems are robust in order to avoid systemic failures — security must be high (e.g. through use of encryption) to build trust.*
- *Successful B2B Exchanges may become regarded as quasi-public utilities and face calls for government regulation (e.g. securities markets after the 1929 Crash).*

Chapter 13:

Secret #5 Add Value by Building a Virtual Community

Although the primary function of an exchange is to provide a centralized pricing mechanism and market space, successful B2B Exchanges will grow beyond this and develop into fully-fledged exchange communities. This means that they will provide the services that allow people in the same vertical to network effectively and to access all the business information they require in one place.

In their groundbreaking book *Net Gain: Expanding markets through virtual communities*, John Hagel III and Arthur G Armstrong made the following observation:

"The rise of virtual communities in on-line networks has set in motion an unprecedented shift in power from vendors of goods and services to the customers who buy them. Vendors who understand this transfer of power and choose to capitalize on it by organizing virtual communities will be richly rewarded with both peerless customer loyalty and impressive economic returns. But the race to establish the virtual community belongs to the swift: those who move quickly and aggressively will gain — and likely hold — the advantage."

In 1997, when they wrote those words, the main impact of the Internet and virtual communities had been in the B2C and C2C space. Most businesses were not embracing the Internet, and the first B2B Exchanges were just being set up. Accordingly, their insights were mainly made in the context of on-line, consumer-oriented communities. However, their insights about setting up virtual communities apply equally to B2B applications.

Successful B2B Exchanges will become powerful virtual communities.

The Six Cs of On-line Services

Steve Case, the CEO of America Online is famous partly for identifying the "Six Cs" that make up a complete on-line service, namely:

- content;
- context;
- community;
- communications;
- connectivity; and
- commerce.

B2B Exchanges must build all of these in order to create a valuable trading community:

- commerce — the centralized market space;
- content — trading data, pricing, product information, industry specific news, etc.;
- context — specialization on a vertical;
- community — value-added services that attract and hold new users;
- communications — the ability for members to meet each other and communicate with each other on-line; and
- connectivity — use of open, web-based applications so that members can use the Internet to connect to the exchange.

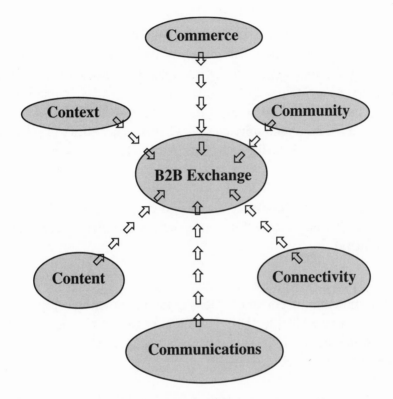

Source: Authors

It is critical that a B2B Exchange does not try to build its own network but rather ensures that all its systems are on the Internet and offers its trading mechanism on the World Wide Web — since these are then open systems that are accessible by all.

Establishing a Trading Community

The first thing an exchange needs to establish is the appropriate trading mechanism (see Chapter 5). This may be as a catalog aggregator, a post and browse model, an auction mechanism, or a fully-electronic auto-matching system.

This centralized market space must be the exchange's core competency.

Next the exchange needs to focus on signing up as many users as possible, as quickly as possible. Only then can the exchange add value by building a community. However, in all cases it is important for the exchange to expand on this core market space capability as quickly as possible. The order of these stages is the direct reverse of the B2C and C2C community model, where it is necessary to establish the community before the members are likely to transact between themselves.

With business-to-business exchange communities, the initial magnet is the commerce function; the community then develops around that.

In the process of signing up users, we have identified the need to smother potential users and signed-up members with customer care and support (see Chapter 10). Excellent customer care is critical in establishing the strength of your brand, creating user loyalty and thus building a sense of community.

In *Net Gain*, Hagel and Armstrong identified three stages of entry in building a community and getting to a revenue-earning position. The first "gate" which a virtual community must pass through is generating traffic (getting target community members to travel to your site). For a B2B Exchange, this stage involves the establishment of the trading mechanism and the sign up of members to trade in the centralized market space.

The second gate involves concentrating traffic (getting them to spend increasing time in the community). For B2B Exchanges, this stage requires the addition of community services that engage the trading members and add value for them, such as:

- fostering relationships and networking between industry players; and
- aggregating trading data, organizing news feeds, and accumulating member-generated content.

The third stage identified by Hagel and Armstrong is locking in traffic (creating switching barriers that make it increasingly difficult for members to leave the exchange community once they have joined). For a B2B Exchange, this third stage involves:

- expanding the exchange's functionality by providing access to third-party services, such as analytical research tools and historical data;
- tailoring the exchange community to individual members' needs by allowing them to customize their experience; and
- integrating member firms' back-office systems with the exchange, or providing back-office logistics within the exchange's web site.

The Economics of Members as Customers

As a B2B Exchange builds the value of its community and starts to lock members into its services, the lifetime value of that member as a customer increases. This means that the revenue stream for the exchange from a member over the lifetime of its membership goes up as the exchange develops into a community.

Conversely, the costs of attracting new customers (i.e. members) will fall sharply as the exchange develops its community. The law of increasing returns means that the exchange with a critical mass of liquidity will attract more new buyers, which attracts new sellers — and so on (see Chapter 10) — without having to increase its marketing or other costs of acquiring new members.

As the lifetime value of each member increases faster for a successful on-line exchange and the costs of customer acquisition fall faster for a successful exchange, the profit margins of the dominant B2B Exchanges will be far higher than in the off-line world.

Enhancing B2B Exchange Community Services

The elements of a B2B exchange community are similar to those which have worked in the B2C and C2C space — after all, businesses are run and managed by individuals — but the focus is on supporting those individuals when they make business decisions rather than their personal spending or lifestyles. The type of services that can be added include:

Industry Rolodex: The primary aim of the community service is to enable users in the same vertical space to network together. In the physical world this normally occurs through specialist magazines, trade shows and conferences. The B2B Exchange can supplement, and even usurp, all of these physical mechanisms. Successful exchanges will add member communication services so that your exchange's address book becomes the "Rolodex" for your vertical market sector.

News Feeds: Another aim of an exchange community is to give managers all the business information they require to do business in that specific vertical through one central resource and to help them process that information more efficiently. This is enhanced by the provision of customized news feeds that are industry-specific (for example, weather forecasts for commodity producers and shipping news for import and export markets). MetalSite provides news and columns from American Metal Market, Metal Center News, and New Steel.

Directory of Relevant Services and Resources: An organized directory of links to other resources on the Network that will assist members of the exchange community, and a directory of buyers and sellers and intermediaries.

Scrolling Ticker: Used to display new bids and offers, postings, trade information and transaction prices, as well as news headlines in real-time. No exchange worth its salt does not have a scrolling ticker.

Bulletin Board: In addition to any trading Bulletin Board, a general Bulletin Board for business networking is often a well-used feature and results in member-generated content.

Discussion Forums: Having empowered buyers through the centralized trading mechanism, it will also be important to allow buyers to communicate with each other, to share experiences and to pass on knowledge gained from dealing with different suppliers.

MetalSite provides discussion forums that are restricted to registered members only. Again this creates member-generated content. These forums should be structured as threaded forums that are monitored by a customer care professional.

Industry Newsletters: The exchange should support its users by producing a customized newsletter every month, including interesting articles from other publications, and by sending members' e-mail messages to alert them to key new information.

Calendar of Industry Events: For example, PaperExchange has an industry calendar of events.

Job Search and Job Ads: PaperExchange enables users to post job listings and résumés, and PlasticsNet maintains a career center.

Classified Ads: This adds to the networking opportunity on the site. PlasticsNet has an active Classified Ads section for members.
Becoming the "Bloomberg" Terminal in Your Vertical

In his autobiographical book *Bloomberg by Bloomberg*, Michael Bloomberg tells the fascinating story of how he set up Bloomberg Financial Services and quickly grew the company into the leading information vendor in the world. At least part of his success is due to his initial focus on the trading of bonds (fixed income securities). Within this vertical, Michael had many years of experience, including being a partner and head of information systems at Salomon Brothers, the large investment bank and bond dealer in New York. Bloomberg developed his terminals with all the historical data, real-time prices, news feeds and yield curve analysis that the average bond dealer required in order to be able to trade effectively. Accordingly, bond-dealing rooms from New York to Hong Kong could be set up around the Bloomberg terminals as the primary information and dealing system.

In much the same way, a B2B Exchange should aim to make its web site the centralized information source, that is, the equivalent of the "Bloomberg" terminal, for that particular vertical. This requires the exchange to ensure, first, that all the real-time pricing and trading data from its centralized market space is readily available to members. This can be achieved by having a "scrolling ticker" on the site and adding customized e-mail alerts that advise members when new prices are posted or trades have been made.

Secondly, the exchange must add streaming news services that are tailored to the needs of traders in that particular vertical. For example, Catex provides a news flash service that highlights any major insured catastrophes and provides a special weather tracking service. In future, it could add live news feed with the latest information and pictures of any insured disasters.

Thirdly, the exchange should build up a database with historical pricing information and provide analytics and research. Analytics are the analytical services that traders require in order to be able to trade more efficiently. These may be specialized pricing models that allow the trader to construct theoretical prices (for example, a Black-Scholes pricing model for options or derivatives), or to test different trading strategies (for example, if he buys so much of product X, how much of product Y must he buy). Research is professional analysis of the market and of market trends which can assist buyers and sellers to assess where the market is headed.

Documents Center

One way of adding value and, at the same time, locking in members, is to standardize the contract terms, terminology and documents used on the exchange in order to grow the market. Incorporating a "documents extranet facility" on the web site can do this. In this documents facility members can post documents for others to access, work on revisions to the contract documents and download documents to their own computers. Sophisticated documents extranets should:

- allow a posting party to specify which other users can see and/or amend a document on the system;
- automatically alert those people that there is a document up there for them;
- track revisions and changes;

- inform the posting party when other users access the documents; and
- provide a library with precedent documents and templates that can be used by members.

By providing precedent documents and helping members to draw up contractual documents on its web site, the exchange can steer the industry towards more standardized forms and terms. At the same time, it can help to lock members in to your exchange whilst building barriers to entry for any potential competitors.

Logistics and Systems Integration

In addition to the centralized market space, a B2B Exchange can offer various centralized back-office and logistics systems, or arrange to host the members' systems on its central hardware.

In the securities world, some smaller stock exchanges have purchased a fully-automated middle- and back-office brokerage system that the exchange then operates on behalf of the broker members. This enables new trading members to get up-and-running quickly, since they do not have to buy their own systems, and ensures that they are committed to staying with the exchange.

For B2B Exchanges that trade physical products, this can include the provision of invoicing, accounting, and purchase order generation services by the exchange (e.g. Chemdex). Enabling users to ship goods, track orders and handle all of the logistics of delivery on-line, through the web-site, also helps to lock users into an exchange.

Sophisticated Financial Services

More sophisticated financial services can be added as the exchange develops, including:

- credit for buyers;
- credit analysis, credit enhancement or credit insurance for sellers;
- payment processing;
- receivables management;

- insurance or warranties;
- shipping, warehousing and inspection services;
- political risk insurance for international trades; and
- foreign currency services to minimize currency risk.

Sophisticated Securities like Derivatives

Successful B2B Exchanges can create indices and develop derivative products that help members to hedge their physical positions or to protect themselves from future price changes.

The first indices can be a historical weighted average of all transactions completed on the exchange for a specific product or a specific term, or in respect of a given region. Initially, the indices should be calculated for the most commonly-traded product or combination of products within each category or region. Once an index has been developed, it can be traded in the form of an options or futures contract in which the value of the derivative contract is based on the level of the index at a specific future time.

For example, Catex may similarly be able to create catastrophe risk indices based on the prices of a given type of reinsurance deal made in their system and to license those indices to insurance companies, investment banks, and/or derivatives exchanges for the trading of options or futures contracts. Those derivative contracts would enable the reinsuring companies to hedge their exposure on the underlying reinsurance contracts.

As the US deregulates electricity along the lines of the Scandinavian model, electricity may become one of the most actively-traded commodities. In this vertical, Houstonstreet and Elinex are vying for market dominance. Traders deal in electricity on a wholesale basis, buying it from power producers and selling to local utilities or to investors who take speculative positions. Each megawatt hour (MWH) produced gets traded many times before it is consumed. Electricity prices can swing from $10 to $1,000 per MWH depending on the temperature, the time of day, and TV viewing habits, such as usage peaks when the whole nation is watching the Super Bowl on TV. In order to smooth out these huge price spikes, producers must manage the risk using derivatives with active participation from major financial market-makers. Elinex's European shareholders have extensive experience in this area.

Elinex is developing Forward Physical Electricity Contracts which enable power producers to hedge their exposure to sudden and dramatic shifts in the price of electricity based on such unforeseeable variables as weather changes or catastrophic events.

This will be a purely financial market for price hedging, risk management, and trade in forward and future power contracts. The trading time horizon is up to three or more years; contracts will be divided into weeks, blocks, seasons, and years.

Accessing Content

Since time to market is critical, a B2B Exchange should not delay its launch until it has all of these community services fully developed; rather, it should launch the basic trading service and seek to "buy-in" or add as many of them as possible, as quickly as possible.

Examples of third-party service providers are:

- networking, forums, scheduling, and other "group-ware" services (eg. Koz.com);
- customized news feeds (Bloomberg, Reuters and industry-specific news sources);
- logistics and supply chain management (e.g. Skyway.com);
- escrow services (e.g. i-escrow.com);
- credit analysis (e.g. ecredit.com);
- document management (e.g. IntraLinks.com); and
- personalized stock tickers (e.g. Yahoo! Finance on PaperExchange.com).

In addition, member-generated content is critical to building a sense of ownership and involvement amongst users.

Member-generated content will come through the addition of Bulletin Boards, threaded discussion forums, and communication services.

User Group Feedback

A B2B Exchange should hold regular meetings of the user groups (see Chapter 12) to get feedback on the systems and the community functions of the exchange.

• • • • • • • • • • • • •

Chapter Summary:

- *Successful B2B Exchanges will be powerful virtual communities.*
- *Start off by establishing the trading mechanism for the centralized market space (e.g. post and browse, or auction).*
- *Sign up as many users as possible, as quickly as possible — then add value by building a community.*
- *Smother the users with customer support.*
- *Add member communication services such as a Rolodex for your vertical market sector, customized news feeds, Bulletin Boards and discussion forums.*
- *Make your web site the centralized information source for your market space — become the "Bloomberg" terminal for your vertical by providing customized news and information services, and by adding transaction data, product information, background analysis, and access to analytics.*
- *Standardize contract terms, terminology and documents used in order to grow the market — build a documents facility.*
- *Link in users' back-office systems, or provide those logistics services through the exchange's web site.*
- *Create indices and develop derivative products that help the users to hedge their physical positions (for example, stock exchanges have created equity indices).*
- *Hold regular user group meetings to get feedback on the systems.*

Chapter 14:

Secret #6 Make the Right Strategic Partnerships

The universality and ease of use of the Internet means that people no longer have to gather on one physical trading floor to create liquidity. However, it is only possible for a new B2B Exchange to challenge an entrenched Industrial Age market if the new entrant can build liquidity at a much lower cost. Increasingly cheap computing power and telecommunications are the weapons that allow Internet-based trading networks to challenge traditional trading mechanisms.

However, the successful exchange must be able to build that liquidity quickly and expand to meet the demand in "Internet time". By far the easiest way of achieving this, as proven by the successful B2C applications, is to work with strategic partners from the very beginning.

Choosing the right strategic partners helps you to scale up quickly in order to achieve domination.

Potential Partners

The potential partners for a B2B Exchange include deep-pocket investors, buyers in the chosen market space, sellers, existing broker intermediaries, new infomediaries, content providers, IT vendors, and trading systems software developers.

However, as described in Chapter 11, it is critical for the exchange to remain commercially neutral. This means that no one user group (for example, buyers, sellers or existing brokers) should be able to control the market.

e-STEEL is a good example of a successful partnership with an IT vendor. After spending months developing the proper business model, e-STEEL chose Computer Sciences Corporation (CSC) as a strategy and technology partner and began a nine-month site development.

Another good example of a successful partnership with an IT vendor is Catex. The original founders of Catex had insurance industry experience, but lacked the IT knowledge to design and build an electronic system for trading risk. To plug this gap, they approached Science Applications International Corporation (SAIC) — an employee-owned software giant that is one of the largest software companies in the US. SAIC had previously designed and built an exchange for trading sulphur dioxide emission certificates and their Internet credentials are strong since they own Network Solutions (the "dot com people"). SAIC became an equity partner in Catex and designed and built the Internet-based trading system that Catex uses.

CreditTrade is an example of a successful partnership with a trading system software vendor. In this case, the software house Mutant Technology, came up with the idea to build an Internet-based trading system for credit derivatives and, based on its CEO's prior experience as head of structured derivatives trading at Barclays De Zoette Wedd, launched CreditTrade.

MetalSite has grown quickly in the steel industry by attracting a number of large steel producers as strategic partners. These sellers have made an equity investment which provided essential capital, but they also brought with them the added liquidity of their business and the credibility that comes from endorsement by key industry players.

Clicks and Mortar Partnerships

In seeking to dominate an on-line vertical, it is sometimes necessary for a B2B Exchange to form a strategic partnership with a traditional bricks and mortar company. Such an alliance has been called a "clicks and mortar" model.

For example, Chemdex has formed a partnership with VWR Scientific Products Corporation, one of the industry's largest distributors of laboratory equipment, chemicals, and supplies to the scientific marketplace. VWR agreed to buy a 10% stake in Chemdex. Chemdex acquired VWR's third-party purchasing service which sourced items that are not part of VWR's catalog range for customers of VWR. *"Chemdex and VWR are a natural fit"*, the press release quotes David Perry, President, CEO and co-founder of Chemdex as stating. *"Successful business-to-business e-commerce requires a marriage of Internet expertise and the ability to move goods in an off-line world."* The partnership is stated to be non-exclusive, allowing Chemdex to maintain its neutral status with other suppliers.

Customize the Market

As part of the laser-like focus and specialization that is required to dominate a particular vertical, a successful B2B Exchange must tailor its applications to the specific needs of its chosen market space.

The best way to achieve this is to work closely with the potentially big users of the exchange and literally "get inside their heads".

Vertical Knowledge

B2B Exchanges are being developed primarily by experienced vertical industry professionals who have seen that, with Internet technologies now being adopted by business, there is an enormous opportunity for them to start up a B2B Exchange. These professionals typically have deep knowledge of their particular industry and strong relationships with the main buyers and sellers in that vertical space. This vertical knowledge is critical in order to build credibility for the exchange within that vertical quickly and to ensure that the exchange is tailored to suit that particular market.

Where a B2B Exchange does not have the necessary level of vertical knowledge on day one, it must move quickly to secure such expertise.

This can be achieved by buying in the experience or by establishing a strategic partnership with a group that does. After some initial success, the founders of PaperExchange realized the critical need for sound vertical knowledge and secured a strategic partnership with a leading industry figure in Roger Stone. Roger Stone became an investor and the Chairman of the exchange.

Vertical knowledge of an exchange and the early sign-up of key industry players are major barriers to entry for potential competitors and ensure that the law of increasing returns apply to that B2B Exchange.

Outsource the Technology

We strongly advise the builders of B2B Exchanges to outsource the technology development. It is critical for a successful B2B Exchange to focus on its core competency — the specific industry expertise that will enable it to create the best business solution possible for that market space — and let the outside technology experts build the systems. For example, e-STEEL, which partnered with Computer Services Corporation.

Although we recommend the outsourcing of the technology build, we also highly recommend that a B2B Exchange buys in the IT expertise of a strong Chief Technology Officer (CTO). One of the dangers faced by all companies in the New Economy is the potential to be "Amazoned". By this we mean the potential for an established business to be "blind-sided" by a new technology that appears, apparently out of nowhere, and that enables completely new start-ups to invade a market space quickly. This is what Amazon.com effectively did to bricks and mortar-based retail bookstore chains in the mid-1990s. An experienced CTO is critical to project manage the outside vendors in the systems build-out and, at the same time, to keep a weather eye out for any tectonic technology shifts.

For the last three years, B2B Exchanges have really had to build their own systems because third-party options were not available. Over the last 12 months, a rash of start-ups have rushed to build and sell the technology for on-line auctions and other exchange functions.

Prominent amongst these are Ariba and Commerce One, who offer E-commerce suites to handle on-line catalog sites; Moai Technologies and OpenSite Technologies for auction-based sites; and Tradex and Tradeum for auto-matching B2B Exchanges. As the B2B Exchange market space expands, the traditional software companies are going to expand their offerings in this area. For example, IBM already has a suite of E-commerce products, and Microsoft has also moved into the on-line auction space with an auction tool kit for its Site Server Commerce software. In addition, some of the specialist stock exchange system vendors, such as OptiMark Technologies, EFA Software, OM Systems and Computershare will soon see the opportunity to re-focus their industrial-strength trading and matching engines from securities markets to other B2B Exchange applications.

Indeed, one of the great opportunities spawned by the growth of B2B Exchanges lies in the provision of technology, marketing, connectivity, content, and consulting services to these new exchange companies.

New Age Thinking

In the Industrial Age, a common approach to project development by companies has been to start by engaging a large firm of outside consultants. The methodology behind this approach is largely based on the belief that it is a mistake to take key senior executives away from their existing jobs in order to develop a new project. Moreover, an outside firm of consultants can approach all interested parties (including potential competitors) and come up with an independent view.

This approach is not ideally suited to the development of a B2B Exchange because B2B Exchanges:

- need to emerge and launch in "Internet time";
- need to have entrepreneurial leadership and be very flexible;
- need to be designed as neutral third-party applications rather than as units within an existing industry player; and
- need very sound vertical knowledge and hands-on industry expertise.

171

Infomediaries

One of the most obvious areas for an emerging B2B Exchange to seek strategic partners is in the development of community services (see Chapter 13). Since the core competency of an exchange is the centralized trading facility, it is unlikely that the exchange will initially have either the resources or the experience to develop many of the potential add-on services that a full community requires.

Sources of reliable historical market data are key potential partners. The value of a trading facility is greatly enhanced by the availability of market data, such as historical prices, volumes, and analytical research services. Whilst this content will develop on the exchange itself as it grows, it may be necessary in the early stages to buy-in the data from the existing traditional market space.

• • • • • • • • • • • • • •

Chapter Summary:

- *Strategic partners help you to scale up quickly in order to achieve domination.*
- *Potential partners include deep-pocket investors, buyers in the chosen market space, sellers, existing broker intermediaries, new infomediaries, content providers, IT vendors, and trading systems software developers.*
- *Work with big users to tailor the market to their specific needs (get inside their heads).*
- *Buy in industry-specific expertise if necessary.*
- *Buy in technology awareness to avoid being "Amazoned" by new technology.*
- *Outsource the technology build.*
- *Avoid large teams of consultants.*
- *Partner with infomediaries who already have data (e.g. historical trade data for securities).*

Chapter 15:

Secret #7 Operate as a Virtual Corporation

In the New Economy the winners will be flexible corporate structures which can "morph" their business plans and innovate in real-time.

In the B2C environment we have seen the business model shift dramatically at least three times in the last four years. Initially, companies sought to charge subscriptions for content on the Web. Then the concept of free content developed, together with attempts to create "portals" that aggregate "eyeballs", with revenue being generated by advertising. Now the emphasis is on driving E-commerce transactions through these portals.

In the UK, the classic business model of AOL, charging monthly subscription fees for Internet access and premium content, has been effectively challenged in 1999 by free ISPs such as Dixon's Freeserve. Now even the staid British Telecom is offering free Internet access in the UK. In order to counter these threats, AOL has had to morph its business plan overnight and offer its own free Internet service in Europe.

In the same way, the B2B space is evolving rapidly and only those companies which are light on their feet will be able to survive.

B2B Exchange companies must be able to move quickly, to innovate, and to scale up fast.

Since B2B Exchanges are a new species of B2B application, the founders of these companies have the opportunity to start with a clean sheet and to adopt the best practices of Internet start-ups. Invariably this means that B2B Exchanges should be "virtual corporations".

Anatomy of a Virtual Corporation

There are eight key guidelines for virtual corporations, as follows:

- concentrate on core competencies;
- outsource the rest;
- remain flexible at all times;
- keep staffing levels low;
- plan to operate on a 24 x 7 basis;
- choose professional advisors who specialize in Internet start ups;
- build partnerships with key corporate leaders; and
- develop strong funding support.

Concentrating on your competency means building the right central market space with a trading mechanism that is tailored to your chosen vertical (see Chapter 6).

Outsourcing the rest means choosing the right strategic partners, who can add value to your core competency (see Chapter 14), or choosing third-party vendors to provide additional services through your exchange.

Remaining flexible means, in part, having teams run the business and adopting virtual communications instead of face-to-face meetings.

Keeping staff levels low is sometimes the most difficult part of being a virtual corporation, but if you outsource vigorously it is possible to keep the full-time staff on the payroll to a minimum. Key full-time staff should include a CEO, COO, CFO, Marketing Head, Customer Support Head and a smart CTO to manage the outsourced IT vendors.

In E-commerce you must be able to operate around the clock, unlike bricks and mortar businesses which operate on a 9 to 5 basis.

An important first step in launching a B2B Exchange is obtaining first-class legal and accounting advice on the design of the market, the rules and regulations of the exchange, and the legal documents for transactions made on the exchange.

Choose a top firm of accountants as auditors, but pressure them to accept low fees for their audit services in the early years. And don't worry about them; they will do very well for fees if and when you go public.

Some service providers and consultants may accept equity in lieu of fees in the start-up phase.

Outsource, Outsource, Outsource

In order to be able to concentrate on the core competency of quickly building a customized trading facility, it is critical that the exchange's staff are not distracted by the need to add other services to the exchange. Outsource everything else, including:

• the technology build;
• the addition of content and community services; and
• the provision of logistics and document processing.

Think Private, Act Public

Smart Internet entrepreneurs establish their businesses as limited liability, private companies, but act as if they are publicly-listed companies from day one.

In the US, publicly-listed companies have to have filed a full registration statement with the Securities and Exchange Commission, conducted an initial public offering (IPO), and been accepted for listing by the NYSE or Nasdaq.

Acting like a publicly-listed company means that you should prepare to go public from day one.

This approach includes:

- hiring the best lawyers and accountants with experience in taking an Internet company public;
- forming "tier 1" relationships;
- having annual audits on your financial statements from the end of the first year;
- having a proper board of directors with an audit committee and a compensation committee; and
- setting up a strong, independent advisory board.

Forming "tier 1" relationships and choosing top professional advisors is critical to building confidence in the exchange and developing the credibility and integrity of the exchange.

B2B Exchanges that want public exposure before conducting an IPO in the US can list on the Mezzanine Market (www.mezzmarket.com) of the Bermuda Stock Exchange (BSX). (Full disclosure: The authors are, respectively, the Chairman and CEO of the BSX.) The Mezzanine Market on the BSX is specifically designed for E-commerce and technology companies to be publicly listed on a recognized stock exchange without the company having to register its securities with the US-SEC and conduct a full initial public offering to retail investors. Instead, investment in the Mezzanine Market is restricted to accredited investors — essentially institutions (such as venture capital funds) and high net-worth investors. Listing on the Mezzanine Market gives a company all of the profile of a public corporation, while also giving the company time to grow until it is sufficiently large enough to justify a full IPO in the US and a listing on Nasdaq or the NYSE.

Customer Care

Exchanges have multiple types of customer and they all demand a very high level of attention. Successful exchanges must focus on marketing to potential customers, since new trading members are particularly essential in the early stages in order to build liquidity on the exchange.

In addition to the usual marketing efforts to secure new members, an exchange must have a thorough customer care and user support program. This must include regular training sessions, a 24-hour, seven-day-a-week help desk, and trading desk facilitators to encourage new listings and trades. These critical employees must get very close to the members and help them to use the system to each member's maximum benefit, and ensure that all the members use the system regularly.

Jurisdiction Shopping

As an Internet-based application, B2B Exchanges must be prepared to position themselves as global players from day one. Where revenues are likely to be generated from all over the world, it makes sense to start off by incorporating a holding company in a leading neutral jurisdiction like Bermuda. Bermuda companies are internationally recognized, and Bermuda is an ideal, neutral jurisdiction that is acceptable to business users all over the world. Bermuda has also implemented the unique Electronic Transactions Act 1999 which creates complete certainty as to the legal validity of contracts formed electronically through web sites such as a B2B Exchange's system.

Funding Options for B2B Exchanges

As with all Internet and E-commerce start ups the initial capital will probably come from the three F's — "family, friends and fools"!

After that, the first and second financing rounds are critical. You must try to choose financial partners who have deep pockets, so that you can tap those partners for the serious money quickly when you need to scale up later.

Business plans should not be too optimistic on revenues to avoid "down rounds" following missed budgets. Venture capitalists (VCs) always build in "ratchet provisions" that can dilute founders significantly in a "down round".

When seeking venture capital, always remember what a VC investor looks for in a B2B Exchange, namely:

- a monster market — but avoid markets with few buyers or dominated by a few sellers (for example, the market for semiconductors — Intel and IBM);
- management experience, including a high level of specific vertical knowledge;
- a market with a complex and fragmented supply chain which a B2B Exchange can simplify;
- a market where buyers and sellers are willing to use technology to create more efficient links between them;
- speed to market (do you have first-mover advantage?);
- scalability; and
- a business model which works, with revenues.

• • • • • • • • • • • • •

Chapter Summary:

- *B2B Exchange companies must be able to move quickly, innovate, and scale up fast.*
- *Concentrate on your core competencies.*
- *Outsource, outsource, then outsource the rest.*
- *Keep staffing levels low.*
- *Prepare to go public from day one — hire the best lawyers and accountants and form "tier 1" relationships.*
- *Have annual audits — choose professional advisors who specialize in Internet start ups and accept equity in the early days in lieu of fees. Force auditors to accept low fees at the start, they will do fine if you go public.*
- *Outsource the technology (e.g. Intralinks with IBM and Lante).*
- *Find a smart CTO to manage the outsource vendors.*
- *Focus on the customers with targeted marketing.*
- *First round financing — after the "family, friends and fools" have invested, try to choose financial partners who have deep pockets. Have the ability to tap partners for the serious money quickly when you need to scale up.*
- *Business plans should not be too optimistic on revenues to avoid "down rounds" following missed budgets.*

Part IV

Future of B2B

Chapter 16:

2B or Not 2B On-line?

Every business must now ask itself, —"2B or not 2B on-line?" That is the question. And our answer is a resounding "Yes!".

The Internet is helping corporate America to re-invent itself and has undoubtedly contributed to five out of the last nine years of continuous expansion in the US economy. Outside of the US, companies all over the world are beginning to integrate the Internet into everything they do. According to a recent study by Booz Allen & Hamilton and the Economist Intelligence Unit entitled *Competing in the Digital Age: How the Internet will Transform Business*, 92% of senior managers at 500 large companies worldwide said they believe that the Internet will transform their business and reshape world markets by 2001 (and 49% indicated that the Internet will have a major impact on their market by 2001).

At times of tectonic shift, everything is revisited and analyzed to see if it can be re-invented. Right now, companies are reviewing how they buy and sell from each other, how they communicate with each other and how they distribute their products to new businesses. In this brainstorming blizzard, B2B Exchanges are very well positioned to become central to all forms of B2B E-commerce.

For companies considering the role of the Internet in their industry a dominant B2B Exchange will be the killer application that lowers their purchasing costs, reduces their inventory levels,

and helps them to keep track of their orders and to expand their market globally.

Size of the Market

In Chapter 2 we identified that the total B2B market space is projected by Forrester Research to hit $1.3 trillion by 2003 and by Goldman Sachs Investment Research to hit $1.5 trillion in value by 2004. With the help of the excellent B2B analysts at Goldman Sachs we have analyzed the role that independent, third-party B2B Exchanges will play in this huge market space. This overall total includes the value of the infrastructure builders — such as the software companies — and the individual storefronts that the largest manufacturers will be able to maintain, in addition to the value that will pass through B2B Exchanges (as we have defined them).

We believe that at least 40% of this trade value will be captured by B2B Exchanges within the next four years, which means that the total value of all transactions made through B2B Exchanges in the US alone will exceed $600 billion by 2004.

Charles Finnie, the senior B2B Internet analyst at the highly respected technology investment bank of Volpe Brown Whelan & Co., has previously stated that "more than half of all B2B on-line trade will flow through such exchanges", so our estimate may be on the low side. If B2B Exchanges can capture revenues representing just 0.5% of this turnover, they will collectively generate $3 billion in revenue per annum by 2004 — and that excludes the rest of the world. Charlie Finnie believes that the gross margins of B2B Exchanges will be as high as 85% and that "B2B Exchanges are the most enormous investment opportunity I have ever seen".

The Internet IS the Strategy

Even the largest and oldest multinationals in the world are now engaged in a headlong rush to integrate the Internet into everything they do. High-level strategic think tanks have been appointed in many of the most well-known industrial companies to try and ensure that they are not "Amazoned" by an Internet-savvy start up. Jack Welch, the 63- year-old Chairman of General Electric Co., is now re-inventing GE from top to bottom under the mantra of "destroyyourbusiness.com". Every division of GE now has a full-time "dyb" team headed by a full-time manager whose task is to re-invent their own business around the Internet before someone else does.

For all companies the Internet should be more than just a communications system. Integrating the Internet into everything that a company does should become every company's strategy.

For some companies this means setting up new units to transfer their products and services on-line. Often these new "dot com" units will actually compete with the Industrial Age divisions, but they are critical in order to ensure that the whole company does not get left behind. For example, Federal Express has an internal unit that is building a totally Internet-based, logistics information handling system to enable companies to communicate more effectively with their suppliers, customers, and shippers. If this new unit is successful it will undoubtedly reduce the amount of information that currently gets passed around between those same parties using traditional FEDEX courier packages.

For other companies, this means spreading their bets and investing in various Internet-based businesses in the hope that one or more of their investments will pay off. For example, in the securities markets of the US, the largest trading members of the NYSE are now busily investing in multiple ECNs and proprietary trading systems. The ECN called Archipelago Holdings, for example, lists Goldman Sachs, Merrill Lynch, J P Morgan, Instinet and E*Trade as investors. At the same time, Goldman Sachs and Merrill Lynch are also invested in Brass Utility and Primex, two other competing ECNs and in OptiMark Technologies, and Goldman Sachs owns more than 16% of Wit Capital. E*Trade is an electronic broker, and Instinet is a form of ECN; interestingly, Instinet is also invested in Tradepoint, an emerging ECN in the UK.

In this environment, B2B Exchanges are ideally placed to secure serious investors. Both Internet-focused venture capital firms and Industrial Age companies that missed out on the B2C "dot com" phenomenon are now exploring business-to-business opportunities on the Internet.

However, key to the success of any B2B Exchange is maintaining independence and neutrality.

Network Megatrends

Underlying the rapid penetration of the Internet into businesses in the US and across the world are two Internet-enabled megatrends. The first is Kelly's New Law of Networks — as set down in Kevin Kelly's book *New Rules for the New Economy*. The second is a shift in power from sellers to buyers.

In the New Economy the value of a network like the Internet actually increases faster than Bob Metcalfe's formula of n^2 (where n is the number of people connected). Kevin Kelly has pointed out that on an electronic Network we can make multiple simultaneous connections between groups of people, so that the potential value of the Network is not just $n \times n$, but n^n.

B2B Exchanges are the most dynamic example of this type of network since multiple buyers and multiple sellers can come together and communicate with each other in a virtual trading space.

The second Megatrend is a shift in the balance of power to the customer. In the B2B world, the Internet has created a "once in a lifetime shift in power" from the companies selling products to their customers — the companies that are buying those products.

B2B Exchanges are the killer application in this Internet Revolution and are creating the dynamic pricing that enables buying companies to significantly lower their acquisition and procurement costs, to lower their inventory levels and to ensure more on-time deliveries to their customers.

Growth Areas and Consolidation

The next year will see a proliferation of new B2B Exchanges being launched. Some of these will compete with, and improve on, the existing exchanges in markets like steel, paper, credit derivatives, electricity and insurance. Others will be launched in completely new markets. Look for new and existing B2B Exchanges to achieve prominence in those industries that have large gross revenues of which a substantial part is currently going to distributors, brokers or intermediaries. It is these markets that will see the most changes as B2B Exchanges develop and enable the manufacturers to avoid much of the intermediaries' fees and the high costs of distribution. For example, PaperExchange has been very successful in the paper industry (a $600 billion gross revenue market in the US alone) because it is a very fragmented market in which the profit margins of the distributors are higher than those of the paper manufacturers.

As we point out throughout this book, multiple exchanges in the same vertical cannot all succeed. The need to dominate and win in a specific vertical will drive many of these competing new entrants to merge.

We therefore predict a period of rapid new growth (12–18 months) and then a period of mergers (18–36 months). The recent merger of PaperExchange and MPX Inc. is just one example of the mergers to come.

Expansion

Successful B2B Exchanges will dominate their chosen vertical markets and then seek to expand into other, closely-related vertical spaces.

Providing that the verticals are closely related there will be obvious advantages in amortizing the exchange's infrastructure across two or more markets.

For example, Skandinavisk Kraftmegling AS (www.skm.se) has achieved a high degree of success in the Scandinavian power markets and is now helping to launch Elinex as an electricity exchange in the US. Similarly, CommerX is now looking to transfer its experiences in developing PlasticsNet to other related verticals and MetalSite has announced plans to expand from just steel products into other metals such as aluminum, copper, and zinc.

B2B Exchange Networking

We maintain a web site at www.b2bexchanges.com that is designed both to keep this book up to date and to form a networking association for B2B Exchanges and interested corporations worldwide. Kevin Kelly's third Law of the New Economy states that "Plentitude not Scarcity" governs the network economy, by which he means that the more networks you are connected to, the more value you can create. B2B Exchanges.com will try to maximise the number of relationships flowing between successful B2B Exchanges.

Feed the Plentitude

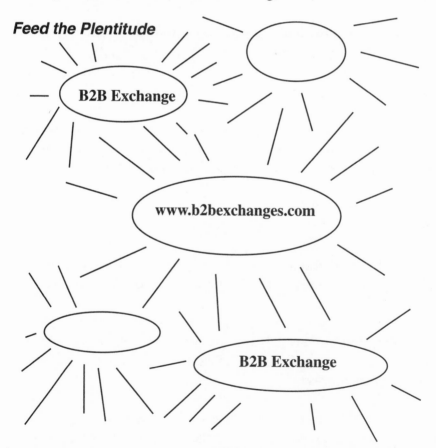

Future of the Securities Industry

In the securities industry we will see a continuing drive towards pan-global trading. But this is most likely to come about through the electronic trading networks linking together to create a "swarm", rather than through mergers of traditional stock exchanges. There are too many conflicting agendas such as systems, personalities and nationalist feelings for traditional, national stock exchanges to work well together. Many of these electronic trading networks will be launched by international broker dealers who wish to internalize their own order-flow and then feed any outstanding orders into a centralized limit order book maintained in an electronic matching engine.

A good example of this new trend is the recently announced deal between Credit Lyonnais Securities Asia (a leading non-US broker dealer) and Bloomberg Financial Markets (which operates a US ECN called "B Trade"). Under this agreement, CLSA will feed their international, non-US order-flow into a global ECN called "G Trade". In this new environment, electronic trading systems will be ideally positioned to become global ECNs in niche markets. For example, the Bermuda Stock Exchange is positioning itself as a well-regulated global ECN for the electronic matching of trades in securities that are not registered onshore with the US SEC (such as the shares of hedge funds and other alternative investment vehicles). Traditional stock exchanges will find it increasingly difficult to compete with these electronic trading networks as they try to link together to form pan-global networks, and the old stock and commodities exchanges will have to rapidly re-invent themselves as "de-mutualized", for-profit, entrepreneurial companies in order to survive.

These electronic, global trading systems will eventually evolve into multi-product platforms — providing markets to trade derivatives, fixed income and traditional equities globally, all on the same system.

All industries should draw conclusions from the fundamental reshaping of the securities business that the Internet and a few order-matching computers have wrought.

Opportunities for Electronic Trading Systems

One of the opportunities being created by the proliferation of B2B Exchanges is in the licensing and sale of electronic trading systems to the exchanges. In this space, the securities market specialists are well ahead of the software firms, such as Tradex and Tradeum, which are currently developing systems for B2B Exchanges. Expect to see firms like EFA Software, OptiMark Technologies and OM Systems – who are providers of sophisticated auto-matching trading systems — moving aggressively into the B2B Exchange market space.

As Dr James Martin points out in his new book *Artificial Intelligence*, software is now being designed in ways that allow the program to evolve and develop a form of machine, or artificial, intelligence. In the near future, sophisticated software agents with artificial intelligence will conduct on-line trading on B2B Exchanges, instead of humans.

A Final Word

In the B2B space, everything is in play. B2B Exchanges are the killer application of this Internet-based revolution for businesses. **May the best exchange win in each vertical!**

• • • • • • • • • • • • •

Chapter Summary:

• *The Internet is helping corporate America to re-invent itself and has undoubtedly contributed to five out of the last nine years of continuous expansion in the US economy.*

• *Size projections for the market space — we predict that B2B Exchange transactions will exceed $600 billion by 2004 in the US alone, with potential revenue for those exchanges of at least $3 billion per annum.*

• *All businesses must re-invent themselves around the Internet (like General Electric Co.). The Internet is more than just a communications medium; it must become the main business strategy.*

• *Metcalfe's Law of Networks has been replaced by Kevin Kelly's new Law of Electronic Networks (n^n). B2B Exchanges are the most dynamic example of this type of network, since multiple buyers and multiple sellers can come together and communicate with each other in a virtual trading space.*

• *In the present environment, B2B Exchanges are ideally placed to secure serious investors from Internet-focused VC firms that missed out on the B2C "dot com" phenomenon and Industrial Age companies that are exploring the Internet.*

• *We give a list of industries where the next B2B Exchanges are likely to develop.*

• *Winner takes most — consolidation is likely as competing exchanges seek to dominate.*

• *www.B2B.exchanges.com is a web site which is intended to update this book.*

• *Future for the securities industry — opportunities for electronic trading systems and broker dealers to be linked together to create a swarm. Traditional stock exchanges will have to re-invent themselves to survive.*

• *Securities trading system software companies will move into the general B2B Exchange space.*

• *In the B2B space, everything is in play.*

Appendix A:

Profiles of Selected B2B Exchanges

Profiles in this Appendix:

- Catastrophe Risk Exchange (CATEX);
- Chemdex Corporation;
- CreditTrade;
- e-Chemicals, Inc.;
- Elinex, Inc.;
- e-STEEL;
- MetalSite;
- National Transportation Exchange;
- PaperExchange;
- PlasticsNet; and
- TechEx.

Catastrophe Risk Exchange (CATEX)

www.catex.com

Overview

CATEX is the only impartial, global, Internet-based trading system for the reinsurance and risk-bearing industry. A licensed reinsurance intermediary, CATEX brings insurers, reinsurers, brokers, self-insureds, and others together over the Internet to match buyers and sellers of reinsurance and to transact reinsurance risks. CATEX facilitates various risks, including environmental liability, marine, aviation, auto insurance, and others. CATEX enables primary insurers and reinsurers to more widely distribute their risks, as well as to diversify the perils they insure against.

History

CATEX was founded in August 1996 by Francis Fortunato, Francis Sweeney, and Samuel Fortunato. Late in 1996, CATEX launched a risk trading system that offered users direct dial access to an ISDN-based private network using a dedicated proprietary software. After Internet technologies began to be adopted in the insurance industry, CATEX introduced a browser-based version of the trading system in November 1998. In December 1999, the company expects to roll out CATEX 2000, an XML-based system developed by Tradeum. CATEX is a privately-held company funded by investments from its founders, Science Applications International Corporation, E W Blanch and Sculley Brothers LLC. CATEX is debt-free and will achieve profitability in Q4'99. The company is currently looking for another round of financing.

Vertical Market Opportunity

CATEX was developed as a means of increasing capacity for coverage against catastrophe. The trading system was well received by the industry and immediately brought greater efficiency and increased the amount of information available to buyers in the reinsurance industry. Because CATEX subscribers have all agreed to anonymously provide information about transactions completed on the system, CATEX is able to offer real-time posting of strike price, deal size, etc. when transactions are completed. Price transparency brings a host of benefits to the industry and fundamentally changes the way reinsurance risks are negotiated and transacted. CATEX, recognizing growing acceptance in the industry, is now beginning to offer large corporate buyers of insurance the ability to check pricing on-line as well as a mechanism to buy directly.

Membership Model

CATEX is a privately-held company controlled by its founders and a group of neutral commercial investors. Membership is open, but is restricted to risk-bearers, their subsidiaries and affiliates. Representatives and firms applying for subscriptions are required to provide documentation confirming their legal status as a risk-bearer or reinsurance intermediary.

Trading Model

CATEX provides a flexible, secure environment for the negotiation of trades using an open "bid and ask" market, or exchange. The speed, efficiency, and flexibility of the CATEX Trading System enables insurers to fashion innovative, integrated risk management strategies and packages. CATEX provides an ideal forum to enable electronic reinsurance transactions involving cash premiums payments, as well as pure risk swaps, and subscribers can use the trading system to sell or purchase traditional reinsurance products such as quota share, per risk excess, or catastrophe excess coverage. CATEX also allows insurers and self-insured companies to purchase reinsurance directly from CATEX subscriber reinsurers. Risk-bearers can diversify their potential liabilities by gaining access to wider risk distributions at minimal costs. Parties are able to respond to listings and negotiate trades by various methods, including CATEX e-mail, real-time text dialog, on-line conferences, collaborative document processing, telephone, fax, or mail. The terms of an agreed trade can be finalized by traditional paper methods or by using the "Deal Mail" facility to construct an electronic proposal or slip. Finally, completed trades are registered with CATEX and the details of the trade are then publicized to all subscribers.

Market Entry Strategy

Before launching CATEX, the founders spent 18 months working with prospective customers to discuss their needs and determine how best to design the proposed trading solution. By leveraging expertise in the industry and focusing on market needs prior to developing a technology platform, CATEX received widespread support from professionals who were willing to buy and sell reinsurance on the electronic exchange. Although CATEX initially focused on catastrophe reinsurance, 60% of postings on the trading system since start-up are for other types of reinsurance. CATEX has not only broadened its range of reinsurance offerings to include more treaty transactions in addition to industry loss warranties, but it has also enhanced its trading platform.

Achieving Dominance

CATEX is the world's largest electronic transaction system for the reinsurance and insurance industries. As of October 1999, CATEX had more than 2,000 postings and had completed nearly 300 transactions representing approximately $1.7 billion in bound coverage and approximately $93 million in premiums. The site is open for trades 24 hours a day, seven days a week, and averages about 8,000 hits a day. All this activity is the result of participation by 148 subscribers and more than 1,600 users registered to trade on the exchange. About 50% of CATEX's subscribers are reinsurers and 20% are brokers. Another 30% are primary insurers and self-insured companies, buyers of reinsurance that CATEX plans to target more directly. To date, the organization has focused its marketing message on insurance companies, reinsurers, and brokers.

"Building a Community" — Services Added to the Trading Mechanism

To provide an optimal analytical environment for informed risk trading, CATEX provides access to critical research tools as well as links to information sources such as insurance and financial news services, ratings and financial data for individual companies, CAT modeling packages, and other specialized risk management data sources. CATEX subscribers can access summary data on completed trades, as well as on-line reports on special topics related to trading activities. The CATEX Document Center enables electronic distribution of entire underwriting submissions of information. CATEX offers subscribers the opportunity to set up a private CATEX network under their own brand. This allows customers to leverage the powerful CATEX trading platform in order to provide on-line insurance trading to their downstream customers and partners without investing large sums on development.

Revenue Model

Subscription fees are CATEX's primary revenue source. Each participating firm pays an annual subscription fee for use of CATEX trading facilities, as well as a trading commission of one-tenth of 1% (ten basis points) of the premium on sale of reinsurance on CATEX. Intermediary fees of 5–15% or 1,000 basis points are typical in the industry. CATEX charges $100 per month for buyers' licenses for primary insurance companies and self-insureds. The buyers' license allows up to ten users on the system. CATEX charges $2,000 per month for sellers' licenses for reinsurers and brokers. The sellers' license allows each member to have 50 employees trade on the exchange.

Confidentiality and Neutrality

CATEX is a New York corporation that is licensed as a reinsurance intermediary acting in a neutral capacity by the New York Insurance Department. The company is subject to oversight and examination by the New York Superintendent of Insurance. CATEX users can use the trading system anonymously until a serious interest in trading is discovered. Following mutual disclosure of the identities of the transacting parties, negotiations proceed in a discreet fashion. CATEX has structured by-laws to assure that no party may improperly obtain trading data, that no sector of the insurance or reinsurance industry is unfairly affected or excluded, and that the integrity and impartiality of CATEX is maintained at all times.

Contact Details for Further Information

Francis Fortunato, CEO
Catastrophe Risk Exchange
26 Broadway
New York, NY 10004
Phone: 1-877-GO-CATEX

E-mail: francisfortunato@catex.com

Chemdex Corporation

www.chemdex.com

Overview

Chemdex Corporation is an exchange and leading provider of business-to-business E-commerce solutions for the life sciences industry. Founded in 1997 in response to the needs of the life sciences industry for a more effective way to manage the procurement of life science research supplies, Chemdex leverages the Internet and E-commerce technology to automate and streamline the entire life science supply chain. The company enables biotech and pharmaceutical companies, as well as academic and research institutions, to efficiently buy and sell life science research products through a secure, Internet-based procurement solution.

History

In 1997, David Perry, President and CEO, founded Chemdex along with Jeff Leane in order to develop a new and more efficient product distribution channel for the life sciences industry. As of October 1999, Chemdex had 170 employees; it completed a $112.5 million initial public offering in July 1999 (Nasdaq: CMDX). Prior to the IPO, Chemdex was financed by major life science and information technology venture capitalists including: Kleiner Perkins Caufield & Byers; E M Warburg, Pincus & Co. LLC; CMG@Ventures; Bay City Capital; Robert Swanson, founder and former CEO of Genentech; and six other life science industry CEOs. Chemdex is not yet profitable. In March 1999, VWR made a 10% investment in Chemdex.

Vertical Market Opportunity

Traditional purchasing methods in the life science industry are inefficient, time-consuming, and costly for the researcher, the enterprise and the supplier. Product orders are traditionally handled through an internal, paper-based purchasing process that requires manual preparation, approval, order tracking, billing, and reporting across multiple departments. The specialized and complex nature of life science research products requires specific and unique knowledge regarding product selection, and fragmentation in the supplier base requires that researchers spend several hours examining multiple paper product catalogs and other information from different suppliers to identify the most appropriate product. The high cost of printing and distributing paper catalogs makes it difficult for suppliers to manage frequent updates and distribution of time-sensitive information.

To effectively address the needs of the life sciences enterprise, a solution must be cost-effective, easily implemented and maintained, enable the enterprise to enforce its particular purchasing policies and business rules, and enable the collection of data to maximize volume purchase discounts and interface to multiple suppliers. To effectively address the needs of the researcher, a solution must be easy to use and provide comprehensive product selection, in-depth product information, specialized search capabilities and efficient ordering and tracking mechanisms. The solution should offer a neutral and fair marketplace with full catalog descriptions of products and product pricing information.

Prominent life science and Internet investors agreed that laboratory supply, with its sophisticated customer base, technical products and high fragmentation, was an ideal market for an Internet-based solution. They funded Chemdex's development and began to assemble a strong management team of industry experts to tackle the supply chain problems of the laboratory supply marketplace.

Membership Model

Chemdex is a public company with semi-open membership. Chemdex sells to individual researchers as well as buyers who are part of an enterprise — all of whom are pre-qualified as valid Chemdex users. Some of the criteria for membership include the need for the registrant to be a member of an official buying organization relevant to Chemdex's market space, scientific research. The registrant should be currently employed by that organization and should show that they will purchase Chemdex products using organization-supplied mechanisms of purchasing, such as a company purchase order or credit card.

Trading Model

Chemdex provides the only end-to-end E-commerce-based procurement solution for the life science industry. Chemdex's procurement solutions combine an extensive on-line marketplace with powerful purchasing capabilities tailored to the unique business needs of each enterprise, as well as comprehensive customer service and support. The Chemdex marketplace is a secure, Internet-based system that enables life science enterprises, researchers and suppliers to efficiently buy and sell life science research products, such as biological and chemical reagents, lab supplies, instruments, and equipment. Chemdex unites enterprises, buyers, and suppliers to streamline business processes, enhance productivity, and reduce costs.

The Chemdex system is based on an expanding database of hundreds of thousands of products, advanced search engines and transaction software that enable users to easily identify, locate and purchase the products they need. The Chemdex solution can also be integrated with third-party enterprise procurement applications and enterprise resource planning systems. Chemdex also provides comprehensive professional services and support for successful deployment, rapid acceptance and usage, and order tracking and fulfilment.

Market Entry Strategy

Chemdex initially focused on building a critical mass of both buyers and suppliers in the life science industry. Chemdex offers suppliers a cost-effective opportunity to reach more customers and sell more products by establishing or enhancing their Internet presence. Chemdex also offers suppliers the capability to implement customer-specific pricing, update product information, and introduce new products without being limited by specific catalog publication cycles. The Chemdex marketplace is supplier-neutral and provides an unbiased comparison of product characteristics and pricing to allow the researcher to make a reasoned choice based upon the information provided by suppliers.

Chemdex intends to continue to leverage its first mover position, expand its offering of leading suppliers and products, and extend its technology leadership with its scalable, robust technology platform. In September 1999, the company announced its intention to acquire Promedix.com, a provider of an on-line marketplace for speciality medical products. The acquisition combines Promedix.com's extensive healthcare industry experience and strong customer and supplier relationships with Chemdex's scalable technology platform and track record of providing end-to-end E-commerce solutions for vertical marketplaces. The acquisition further strengthens Chemdex's position as a leader in B2B E-commerce and will enable Promedix.com to accelerate its time to market with a solution for the healthcare industry.

Achieving Dominance

As of June 1999, Chemdex had approximately 49 customers including pharmaceutical and biotechnology companies, as well as academic institutions. Chemdex markets and sells its solutions through a combination of a direct sales force, an internal telemarketing sales force and strategic partners such as VWR (VWR Scientific Products Corporation, one of the industry's largest distributors) and BIO (the Biotechnology Industry Organization). This sales and marketing approach is designed to help customers and suppliers understand both the business and technical benefits of the Chemdex solution, and to promote user adoption through one-on-one education and training. Chemdex participates in seminars, direct mailings, trade shows, speaking engagements, and web site marketing. In addition, comprehensive PR and marketing programs are used to educate, convert and train researchers and purchasing agents to use Chemdex for their life science research product orders.

Revenue Model

Chemdex revenues are based on a combination of transaction fees and software application licensing fees.

Confidentiality and Neutrality

Chemdex is a vendor-neutral marketplace committed to customer privacy.

Contact Details for Further Information

Chemdex Corporation
1500 Plymouth Street
Mountain View, CA 94043
Phone: 1-650-813-0300

E-mail: info@chemdex.com

CreditTrade

www.creditrade.com

Overview

CreditTrade is an Internet exchange designed to allow financial institutions to trade and manage credit risk. CreditTrade hopes to become the least expensive way to trade credit, costing nothing to use or access unless a trade is completed and negotiated through the site, when a commission will be charged. The credit derivatives marketplace is currently hindered by a lack of transparency and a shortage of standardized documentation. CreditTrade delivers solutions to these problems by dramatically improving the ease, transparency and efficiency of institutions to exchange documents, negotiate, trade, and manage credit risk. It also offers a comprehensive picture to all credit traders concentrating on credit derivatives, loan trading, and other structured credit trades. CreditTrade was initially funded by Mutant Technology. Although there have been no revenues to date, the first trade closed on 21 September 1999. CreditTrade is currently raising Series B funding.

History

London-based Mutant Technology was formed to exploit Internet technologies in the wholesale financial sector. Out of Mutant Technology, the idea behind CreditTrade took hold in January 1999. Founded by Paul Ellis, it was initially started and operated as part of Mutant Technology. CreditTrade was then formed as a separate company in September 1999. CreditTrade.com was initially launched on a trial basis with simulated trading on 30 June 1999. The official launch with live trading was on 26 July1999.

Vertical Market Opportunity

In 1998, the British Bankers' Association estimated that the global credit derivatives market was $350 billion. This huge market was not being specifically targeted by any one party, and was well understood by CreditTrade's founders. There is a crowded E-commerce marketplace for fixed income, bonds and other commoditized retail products. The systems to deal with and settle these commodities are more easily understood and created. The credit marketplace is not commoditized; revenue depends on details of the trade that must be negotiated. Because of this, it is less easily understood and solutions are less easily implemented, which results in a less crowded marketplace.

There are two primary reasons why credit trading is well suited for the Internet — documentation and transparency. Because the Web can be used to automate the occasionally extensive documentation required to define and close credit transactions, sharing between business partners can be streamlined. The CreditTrade web site provides a mechanism to upload, download, share, and forward documents involved in negotiating and closing a deal.

In addition, the Web offers transparency, which is an improvement over the traditional system where brokers intermediate between different market players. Before the Web introduced real-time communications, not everyone had access to all the information that might be available at any given time. Before CreditTrade, when trades were done, brokers had privileged information that became valuable when they talked to another market player. This presented problems of favoritism and decreased market liquidity; players who didn't feel they were "in the loop" were less likely to take risks. The CreditTrade web site introduced an "electronic broker" that is efficient, transparent, and neutral. The most important thing the Web does here is to bring transparency to the credit trading marketplace with the goal of increasing volume.

Membership Model

CreditTrade is commercially-owned with an open, but qualified, membership policy. All, members are thoroughly evaluated before they can trade on CreditTrade. The compliance process includes verification of identity, as well as verification that users are members of a regulated institution in good standing. Because the financial markets are regulated in the UK by the SFA (an agency like the SEC in the US), CreditTrade is looking to the stock markets for examples as its membership model continues to evolve.

Trading Model

CreditTrade implements a post and browse system giving users the ability to constrain what details can be viewed by other users. The post and browse system is enhanced and automated with the use of templates designed for different users. Deals are described and posted, then users can search the CreditTrade database to find deals that match their needs.

If traders see a trade that interests them, they can correspond anonymously with the person who posted the trade. If they reach an agreement, then, provided each party agrees, CreditTrade will effect a simultaneous exchange of names allowing completion of the trade directly. The parties then "lock" the deal on the system and clear credit and/or finalize the documentation off-line. Once a trade is executed, it must be reported back to the exchange. If the trade does not get executed off-line, then the parties can "unlock" the trade on the system. Once a trade has been executed, that information is collated and published on the site to provide a price reference for other participants. CreditTrade is also expanding the trading system to provide a new "customer deals" area where banks can provide deals directly to their customers via the CreditTrade site. The bank gives CreditTrade a list of people who are allowed to see various deals. CreditTrade does not charge the banks on a deal-by-deal basis, but charges a membership fee for the privilege of using the bulletin board system.

Market Entry Strategy

CreditTrade gets in the middle of the deal flow, that is, it "oils the engine of transactions". The market entry strategy was primarily to focus on the credit derivatives market as a subset of the larger and more crowded credit trading sector.

Achieving Dominance

CreditTrade has a growing base of traders. Marketers on staff at CreditTrade make on-site visits to encourage users to post trades and also to help facilitate closing trades.

"Building a Community" — Services Added to the Trading Mechanism

Over the past two-and-a-half years, Mutant has developed a variety of technologies to power on-line trading systems. Much of this functionality has been incorporated into the CreditTrade exchange. In addition, CreditTrade uses Reuters news to provide credit industry news on the site, and has a partnership with Market Abilities Unlimited to provide information and education about credit products, a resources section of the site, and forums for commentary about what is happening in the credit trading market.

Revenue Model

CreditTrade's revenues will come from a combination of transaction commissions, membership fees and subscription fees. If a trade gets done on the anonymous trading site as a result of a CreditTrade introduction, then a commission is collected based on the size of the deal. CreditTrade would not specify the amount of the commission charged, but did indicate that it will almost always be less than a normal broker commission. In the customer area of the site, membership fees are charged for use of the bulletin board site. These fees are based on overall trading volume and no per deal transaction commissions are charged. Subscription fees are collected for access to market information generated by the trading mechanism in certain cases.

Confidentiality and Neutrality

All deals and communications on CreditTrade are anonymous. In addition, all data is encrypted, so traders can be confident that any information sent cannot be intercepted. Although anyone can get a password to access the site, to view, post, and respond to trades, a "trader" status is required. Neutrality is ensured because the exchange is widely held by an investment group.

Contact Details for Further Information

CreditTrade
12/13 Henrietta Street
London, WC2E 8LH
United Kingdom

E-mail: paule@mutant-tech.com

e-Chemicals, Inc.

Overview

e-Chemicals is a leading E-commerce chemical marketplace that facilitates the secure and rapid procurement, sale, and delivery of industrial chemicals. The company's web site www.e-chemicals.com, offers an integrated solution that allows buyers to select a product, get a price, and order and track shipments on-line. e-Chemicals also provides customized E-commerce-based procurement solutions for corporate purchasing organizations that provide machine-to-machine connectivity and dramatically streamline the procurement process.

History

e-Chemicals was founded in the fall of 1998 by Alf Sherk, Lorne Darnell and Yossi Sheffi. The site was launched in November 1998. Headquartered in Ann Arbor, Michigan, e-Chemicals is owned by its founders, employees, and holding company Internet Capital Group (Nasdaq: ICGE). e-Chemicals has been generating revenue for less than a year and is focused on gaining first mover advantage. Because of this, the company is continually investing in expanding the offering and acquiring customers, and is not yet profitable.

Vertical Market Opportunity

e-Chemicals was established to address the challenges facing chemicals industry purchasing professionals who are constantly torn between two competing objectives: implementing supplier initiatives aimed at improving efficiency, and enlarging the vendor base to lower unit costs through increased competition. Solving this challenge of the fragmented chemical supply market is the driving principle behind e-Chemicals. e-Chemicals' management team has more than 150 years of collective experience in chemical logistics, manufacturing, and distribution. The company relies on this industry expertise and insight into the supply chain challenges of the chemicals industry to deliver integrated solutions for the industry, and then partners with distributors and suppliers to enable these companies to offer an E-commerce solution to their customers. e-Chemicals first concentrated on on-line commerce, enabling customers to facilitate a purchase from order to delivery through one transaction. The company then enhanced its services by introducing dynamic pricing tools such as auctions.

Membership Model

e-Chemicals is a privately-held company. Membership is limited to qualified buyers and suppliers of industrial chemicals.

Trading Model

e-Chemicals launched its web site with a multi-vendor catalog and recently added seller-driven auctions. The company is also adding automated requests for quotations to their e-procurement solutions offering. e-Chemicals integrates the benefits of increased access to new sources of supply and new negotiating tools with order fulfilment and financial settlement, to provide a streamlined solution to the chemical industry's supply chain inefficiencies. e-Chemicals provides financial settlement through Sun Trust and logistics through Yellow Services. Customers can review their order on the web site at any time to determine its status.

Market Entry Strategy

e-Chemicals' initial focus was exclusively on the industrial chemical segment. The company's first priority was to develop an integrated, on-line business model that enables the company to serve as a neutral channel for both the supplier and the customer to execute the secure and rapid procurement, sale, and distribution of industrial chemicals.

e-Chemicals believes that E-commerce will be an integrated component of a multiple channel distribution process, and has designed its service to adapt to the needs of individual procurement professionals. This year e-Chemicals expanded its offering to include e-procurement solutions for large corporate chemical buyers. Specifically, e-Chemicals works with the purchasing organizations to streamline the procurement process by eliminating as many steps as possible and automating the rest. The next step is to focus on strategic sourcing initiatives, such as aggregation of demand and the implementation of dynamic pricing tools. e-Chemicals' ultimate goal is the integration of its E-commerce system with its customers' ERP systems.

Achieving Dominance

As of October 1999, e-Chemicals had more than 1,000 products listed on its site and had registered 600 buyers, as well as 20 manufacturers and suppliers. e-Chemicals markets itself aggressively through a variety of marketing and sales strategies. Ads placed in chemical trade publications focus on customer acquisition. The company's retention marketing efforts include follow-up communications via e-mail for new customers who have subscribed to the site, as well as direct mail pieces and invitations to special events such as auctions. e-Chemicals' corporate communications efforts consist of media relations, industry analyst relations, and executive speaking circuit programs. e-Chemicals has a dedicated, direct sales force to sell its e-procurement solutions to large customers and suppliers and targets small customers through telemarketing and direct marketing efforts. e-Chemicals also gains market strength through key industry partnerships with the Synthetic Organic Chemical Manufacturers' Association (SOCMA) and the National Association of Chemicals Dealers (NACD). In addition, the company leverages technology and logistics partnerships with IBM, SunTrust, and Yellow Services.

"Building a Community" — Services Added to the Trading Mechanism

e-Chemicals provides daily industry news and features reports on critical issues that impact the chemicals market and E-commerce industry. A news archive and web site demo are also available for those who are not familiar with e-Chemicals and its ordering process. A feedback mechanism on the site permits customers to submit questions, and a customer service call-in number is also posted on the site. e-Chemicals is in the process of adding services such as document management and compliance reporting to meet environmental, health, and service regulations.

Revenue Model

e-Chemicals takes title to the products it sells and bills the customer directly. For small customers, e-Chemicals buys the products and resells them with a mark-up; large customers are charged transaction fees.

Confidentiality and Neutrality

e-Chemicals is a neutral marketplace. Access to e-Chemicals' high-security web site is limited by user name and password, and all customer registration information and order data is encrypted for secure transactions. This security, coupled with the company's published confidentiality policy provides customers with a high level of assurance that their data will not be misused.

Contact Details for Further Information

e-Chemicals
505 East Huron, Suite 208
Ann Arbor, MI 48104
Phone: 1-734-827-3411

E-mail: info@e-chemicals.com

Elinex, Inc.

www.el-in-ex.com

Overview

Elinex is a wholesale marketplace for buyers and sellers to trade electricity; it also provides analytical tools and real-time market information. A leader in the highly-competitive marketplace for bilateral forward and futures electricity contracts, Elinex provides services for participants in the electric power markets that include contracts, risk management, education, training, and consulting. Elinex is a privately-held company headquartered in Massachusetts. Initially funded by the founders and reliant on a strategic technology partnership with the largest exchange of this kind in Europe, Elinex is now closing Series A funding from a group of strategic investors representing both industry expertise and capital.

History

In 1998, California became the first state to deregulate electricity. The rest of the country was quick to follow and today all but two states have deregulation laws in progress. The deregulation of the electric power industry opens the door to one of the largest commodity markets in the world. Yet with this tremendous opportunity comes the risks associated with any freely-traded market. Because of this, electric power industry participants need access to a liquid market that provides long-term hedging instruments.

Aware of the issues presented by deregulation, Petter M Etholm and Borge Bogaard founded Elinex. Petter and Borge spotted an opportunity to transform the US electricity industry by providing a full-service marketplace for trading electricity in the Eastern Power Grid. Drawing expertise from a strategic partnership with Skandinavisk Kraftmegling, AS (SKM), Elinex is able to leverage systems and practices already proven effective in the Scandinavian electric markets, which began deregulation in 1991.

215

Vertical Market Opportunity

A background in international trade trained Petter to look for markets developing in one part of the world that had not yet spread to other areas. This allowed business practices to be tested and refined in early markets, then rapidly translated to other markets with a high probability for success. Norway deregulated its electric power industry in 1991; Sweden deregulated its market in 1994. Deregulation of US electricity markets beginning in 1998 presented Petter and Borge with the opportunity they were looking for: a proven business model in one part of the world that could be translated to another large market.

They acquired additional industry expertise for Elinex through a strategic relationship with SKM. With SKM, Elinex has years of proven experience providing an electricity marketplace to the Nordic market, one of the most mature deregulated electric markets in the world. SKM began operations in 1992, shortly after the deregulation of Norway's electric power industry. Early operations as a power broker quickly evolved into a marketplace for SKM's standardized forward electricity contracts, providing Norway's energy buyers and sellers with specialized hedging, speculation, and physical delivery instruments. Significant components of the Nordic market have been used as a model for Elinex's trading platform.

Membership Model

Elinex is owned by commercial investors and has open membership policies. A commitment to neutrality was reflected in Elinex's fundraising. In order to be perceived as impartial and neutral, Elinex ensured that there was no ownership by American utility companies, generators, or other market participants. Elinex's membership is strictly controlled. Participants must be qualified professionals from prescreened companies that are required to prove creditworthiness and, if participating in physical markets, must demonstrate the ability to take or make delivery.

Trading Model

The Elinex marketplace uses a post and browse system to match buyers and sellers of electricity based on their trading requirements. Because credit is a big concern in the electric industry, most participants have a list of companies they are permitted to trade with. Elinex automatically finds matches within the approved list. Once an introduction is made, negotiations take place via phone or chat room. All communications are anonymous until parties choose to release their identities. Although all connections are currently made via phone, the Internet-based solution will be launched in December 1999.

Elinex hopes to offer the most liquid electricity marketplace for both standardized and non-standardized products. Standardized contracts are well defined with regards to terms, delivery point, price indexing, load profile, etc. Non-standardized or tailor-made contracts are also traded frequently and differ from standardized contracts in one or many aspects. They can be as long as 10-20 years, or as short as a few days.

Market Entry Strategy

For strength in the marketplace, Elinex relied on strategic partnerships both to leverage technology and industry expertise and to ensure liquidity. Through an exclusive bilateral licensing agreement, Elinex shares information, technology and computer systems developed by SKM. This gives Elinex a tremendous edge in the US power market. Because electricity is not a commodity that "sticks around", it is important to have both buyers and sellers participating at the same time. To guarantee market liquidity and ensure that deals could be closed, Elinex initially targeted market-makers and special deals were negotiated with those who were willing to continually have spreads available.

Achieving Dominance

Elinex now has 20 users, including generators, power plants, utilities, large and mid-size industrial loads, consumer groups that can now buy power wholesale, co-operative buying groups, and public interest groups. Membership is balanced between buyers and sellers. In order to close the complicated deals that are typical of the electricity marketplace, Elinex account executives must understand the physical limitations of the power grid as well as the financial options available. Credibility, industry contacts, and knowledge are essential, and Elinex relies on a staff with years of utility trading experience. Elinex draws new customers to the trading system one-by-one, using a combination of activities including sales calls, seminars, speeches at industry conferences, and public relations activities.

"Building a Community" — Services Added to the Trading Mechanism

Elinex's trading system automatically confirms trades and sends invoices for transaction fees. Working with SKM and other strategic partners, Elinex also provides users with analytical tools and related consulting services including one of most sophisticated price forecasting models in the electric industry, market information generated by the trading system and risk management practice consulting.

Revenue Model

Elinex's primary revenues are generated from transaction fees that are charged as a percentage of each deal facilitated by the system. Elinex plans to charge subscription fees for analytical tools such as the pricing model, as well as for market information and statistical data generated from the electricity marketplace.

Confidentiality and Neutrality

Elinex is a neutral marketplace that enables anonymous trading of electricity. Currently, Elinex matches offers and buyers via phone, regulated by internal rules. An Internet-based trading site will automate anonymous trading, guarantee first-in-first-out execution, and perform clearing functions. Elinex does not take title to traded electricity. Elinex screens prospective members to ensure financial standing.

Contact Details for Further Information

Elinex, Inc.
Post Office Box 3595
Peabody, MA 01960
Phone: 1-888-9elinex (888-935-4639)

E-mail: petholm@el-in-ex.com

e-STEEL

<u>www.e-STEEL.com</u>

Overview

e-STEEL is a business-to-business exchange that allows companies to buy and sell steel products over the Internet. e-STEEL serves the global steel market and supports all prime and non-prime steel products including hot rolled, cold rolled and coated sheet, plate, tin mill, and rebar. e-STEEL plans to add pipe and tube, wire rod, structural and other steel product by early next year. e-STEEL provides the steel industry with both a neutral, secure on-line exchange and rich, up-to-date industry information. Suppliers use the e-STEEL exchange to expand their marketing reach, grow their customer base, provide faster, more efficient customer service to existing commercial partners, and reduce transaction costs. Buyers expand their supplier base, find better prices, and lower purchasing costs. In June 1999, venture capital investors Bessemer Venture Partners, as well as Kleiner Perkins Caufield & Byers and Greylock provided a combined $10 million in initial funds. In September 1999, Comdisco provided $6 million in equity and sub-debt. Since e-STEEL only launched in September 1999, the company is not yet profitable.

History

For almost a decade, e-STEEL founder, Michael S. Levin envisioned setting up a 24-hour international electronic market place to buy and sell steel. He recognized that the Internet presented a solution to many of the business problems that plagued the metals industry and founded e-STEEL in September 1998. After spending months developing the proper business model, e-STEEL chose Computer Sciences Corporation (CSC) as a strategy and technology partner and began the nine-month site development. In the spring of 1999, e-STEEL began testing and simulated trading. e-STEEL began accepting new membership applications at the end of July 1999. The first trade involving prime hot rolled steel was closed between Cargill and

Worthington Industries, shortly after the formal launch of the e-STEEL exchange in September 1999.

Vertical Market Opportunity

Although steel is the second-largest global industry, it had no central marketplace. The fragmented market made it difficult for buyers and sellers to find each other. Phones, faxes and paper-intensive documentation created high transaction costs. The industry lacks transparency and faces tremendous profitability challenges. Steel industry leaders believed E-commerce to be a way to streamline purchases and better serve their customers, yet there was no clarity regarding how and when E-commerce solutions would be adopted. After working in several segments of the steel industry for 25 years, Michael S Levin had access to CEOs and other decision makers and began to gather information from them to determine what type of solution was needed. Relying on his industry experience, Levin gained early participation by companies willing to invest the time to see whether e-STEEL's solution worked for them. Through this collaborative testing and evaluation process, e-STEEL learnt what the system needed to do, was able to see what worked, and determine what additional features were needed.

Membership Model

e-STEEL is a neutral marketplace owned by commercial investors. To become an e-STEEL member, companies must be legitimate participants in the global steel market. Buyers and sellers of steel must pass a qualification process, which includes a credit check and corporate profile.

Trading Model

e-STEEL operates on a negotiation basis between buyer and seller which can be initiated by either side. For instance, a buyer could make an offer on a selected product. The seller could award it or make a counter-offer. The buyer could accept the counter offer or make one of his own. Sellers may list products for sale directly over e-STEEL. e-STEEL notifies members that a product has been sold either through confidential e-mail or fax. e-STEEL does not change the claims process. Sales contracts between the buyers and sellers continue to regulate transactions. All transactions are fully documented on the e-STEEL system and e-STEEL monitors compliance with exchange rules. The foundation of the e-STEEL exchange is a combination of electronic commerce and personalization software that enables users to check product availability, post orders, and buy and sell steel. A proprietary customization application called STEELDIRECT ™ provides buyers and sellers with the power to mirror existing relationships, pricing structures, and distribution arrangements on the Web.

Market Entry Strategy

The metals industry is pyramidal with about 200 large companies producing 700 tons of product per year for an estimated million end users worldwide. e-STEEL targets the large steel producers, as well as all of the subsequent buyers and sellers of steel in the complex steel value chain as it works to build traction. By addressing the needs of those at the producing end of the chain, e-STEEL hopes to become an indispensable vehicle that can facilitate more cost-effective transactions with others segments of the supply chain. Because it is inefficient and costly to reach the majority of end-user companies in the supply chain, large suppliers have prioritized the need to develop streamlined E-commerce solutions for this segment. e-STEEL believes that by handling transactions and logistics electronically, the costs of doing business can be significantly reduced, and that this will motivate the top producers to help drive adoption through the rest of the supply chain.

Achieving Dominance

Just four weeks after launch, e-STEEL already had more than 200 member companies. e-STEEL is focused on attracting business that can be transacted more cost effectively, delivering the ability to make it easier and quicker to buy and sell, and empowering steel professionals to gain efficiencies with their existing customers. In the metals industry, E-commerce is intellectually readily accepted, but has not yet gained critical mass. Recognizing that it may be 18 months or more before there is industry-wide adoption, e-STEEL is focused on implementation, testing, security, and ensuring scalability. The right business model, the right financial backing, and the strength of industry experience are e-STEEL's competitive advantages. The company is able to match the pace of the industry and is ready to take advantage of any opportunity to deliver more efficient, one-stop-shopping.

"Building a Community" — Services Added to the Trading Mechanism

e-STEEL provides industry and trade news, job listings, and stock data and is working with technology partners such as Silknet, Broadvision, and CSC to deliver supply chain and purchasing system integration solutions. e-STEEL is developing systems that in the future, will allow buyers to negotiate credit terms on-line and to authorize e-STEEL to pay the seller. In addition, buyers will be able to connect with e-STEEL's logistics partners to arrange delivery, once a transaction is negotiated. Because user searches, purchases and company information are all remembered, buying processes become automated which increases time savings and makes the e-STEEL solution more valuable the more it is used. To attract senior professionals as well as buyers, e-STEEL may publish a prime steel index from transaction information gathered from the trading site.

Revenue Model

e-STEEL charges sellers a transaction fee of less than 1% on all purchases initiated on the site, though payments between commercial partners occur off-line. Because e-STEEL wants to provide a "frictionless" marketplace for the entire global steel industry, there are no membership, subscription, or posting fees. In the future, e-STEEL may charge fees to suppliers that want to set up storefronts with exclusive supplier information.

Confidentiality and Neutrality

e-STEEL is neutral; it does not own any of the products transacted on the system, and is not affiliated with any industry participant. All information is kept in the strictest confidence, and all participants are treated fairly in order to guarantee high satisfaction levels, as well as to encourage trading activity.

Contact Details for Further Information

e-STEEL Corporation
1250 Broadway, 30th Floor
New York, NY 10022
Phone: 1-212-527-9997

E-mail: info@e-STEEL.com

MetalSite

www.metalsite.net

Overview

MetalSite is a neutral and secure Internet marketplace for buying and selling metals products. It also serves as a comprehensive industry resource for news and information. For metals buyers, MetalSite is a comprehensive resource for up-to-date information about their industry and the products being offers by manufacturers. For sellers, MetalSite presents an opportunity to expand their customer base, increase efficiencies in the selling process, turn over inventory more quickly, and free up the sales force from non-value-added tasks.

History

MetalSite was initiated in 1996, when founder and CEO Patrick Stewart was asked to develop an Internet strategy for his employer, Weirton Steel Corporation, the eighth-largest steel producer in the US. Stewart and his team of experts recognized the tremendous inefficiencies that existed along the entire metals supply chain and saw the Internet as a cost-effective solution to these inefficiencies. Using Weirton Steel as a test site and proving ground for the concept of buying and selling steel products on-line, Stewart made an initial investment of $3 million to conduct extensive research and testing, before launching the MetalSite marketplace in 1998. MetalSite is a privately-held, limited partnership. Initial investors included industry participants LTV Steel, Steel Dynamics, and Weirton Steel Corp. In September 1999, industry giants Bethlehem Steel and Ryerson Tull joined as new investors. MetalSite's current investors represent nearly 22% of steel shipped in the US annually. MetalSite expects to be "cash neutral" by the end of its second year of operation.

Vertical Market Opportunity

Although the world metals industry produces 750 million tons per year, the largest US producer claims only 10% market share. MetalSite's founder, Patrick Stewart, is a steel industry veteran who saw an opportunity to streamline the inefficient and fragmented metals supply chain. He recognized that the Internet provides a real-time communications network that can centralize and streamline the inefficient and complex network of buyers.

The MetalSite think-tank reviewed thousands of pages of information about the Internet, E-commerce, and the steel industry and then conducted customer interviews and surveys to gather information used to determine the structure of the web site. This research was supplemented by discussions with experts, including: Thomas Malone, MIT professor and an early theorist on the impact of electronic marketplaces; Mark Teflian, creator of the Apollo airline reservation system and current CTO for Perot Systems; and the Doblin Group, a world leader in creating user-driven strategy concepts. The research, especially that conducted by the Doblin Group, focused on steel buyers' behavior and helped determine how the marketplace should be designed as well as how MetalSite could be effectively marketed.

Membership Model

MetalSite is a privately-owned limited partnership of industry participants. Although initially funded in part by the steel industry's largest producers, MetalSite offers open membership and has gone to great measures to provide a neutral marketplace and to ensure that customers' information is kept strictly confidential. Visitors must complete a buyer's profile before they may enter the on-line marketplace. MetalSite verifies the legitimacy of the buyers, and creditworthiness is determined by the seller.

Trading Model

The MetalSite marketplace offers a wide range of options for buying and selling prime and non-prime products and provides a single point where users can easily and cost-effectively locate and purchase products from multiple companies on-line. The MetalSite catalog includes a product guide and sealed-bid auction. The product guide supports a price list, contract pricing, volume discount pricing and on-line negotiations. Prime and non-prime products are offered in an auction format, utilizing traditional channels for payment and logistics. Sellers can solicit bids, privately review them and then award the sale. Bid solicitation, submission, and award are all conducted privately via MetalSite.

Market Entry Strategy

In order to build a successful marketplace that would attract buyers, MetalSite initially secured commitments from major steel producers to commit inventory on a daily basis and to list a substantial volume of product for sale monthly. These steel suppliers were leaders and innovators in the national and international marketplace and brought both credibility and product to the MetalSite marketplace. MetalSite continues to recruit new sellers in order to ensure that buyers will participate in trading.

MetalSite built the web marketplace in strategic phases, launching with content and community services, then adding E-commerce capabilities. Initially, MetalSite offered excess prime and secondary products via a low-risk, sealed-bid auction format for buyers and sellers. Later, products and services were expanded to include prime and made-to-order products in a catalog format supporting a list price, contract pricing, volume discount pricing and on-line negotiations. Services such as banking, logistics, and on-line order status were added, and electronic purchase orders, bill collection and bill payment systems were also introduced. The next phase of implementation will expand product offerings to include other metals such as aluminium, copper, and zinc, and will make available unparalleled industry reports created from the purchasing data generated by the electronic marketplace.

Achieving Dominance

MetalSite currently has more than 1,200 buyers and thousands of registered associates. MetalSite has grown from three initial sellers to a projected 40 by the end of 1999. Monthly product volume has grown from 20,000 tons to more than 120,000 tons, representing more than $45 million worth of product available for sale at the MetalSite marketplace on a monthly basis. MetalSite's marketing programs include print and on-line trade advertising, aggressive media relations activities, one-on-one sales, participation in, and sponsorship of, industry events as well as speaking engagements.

"Building a Community" — Services Added to the Trading Mechanism

The MetalSite marketplace delivers all the services required to research an order, to find a product, and make a selection, to order and track product, and to pay and settle the order. Other services MetalSite plans to implement in 1999 include banking services such as electronic billing and credit options; accounting services such as on-line order status and an electronic purchase order system; and a logistics program that offers a range of tracking and transportation features.

Revenue Model

Buyers can access and use the site for free. Sellers are charged a transaction fee ranging from 1/4% up to 2% for each on-line sale. In addition, MetalSite offers consulting services for the development of an individual market center that basically is a mini-web site for vendors that want to be represented on the MetalSite marketplace. Advertising sponsorships and banners are also available.

Confidentiality and Neutrality

Security and confidentiality are extremely important issues at MetalSite. The Arthur Andersen Risk Management group audits MetalSite's business practices, policies, and procedures every six months. A copy of the audit and the MetalSite business practices are published on the MetalSite homepage for access by all visitors. MetalSite also requires that all employees sign a confidentiality agreement legally binding them to comply with the company's strict rules of confidentiality and business practices as a condition of employment.

Contact Details for Further Information

MetalSite
Penn Center West
Building Two, Suite 200
Pittsburgh, PA 15276
Phone: 1-877-246-4900/1-412-490-4900

E-mail: info@metalsite.net

The National Transportation Exchange

<u>www.nte.net</u>

Overview

The National Transportation Exchange (NTE) is an electronic transportation marketplace which utilizes Internet technology to provide shippers, third-party logistics companies, and motor carriers with a trusted electronic network that eliminates supply chain inefficiencies and improves the productivity and profit margins of its members. NTE connects shippers who have loads they want to move efficiently with fleet managers who have space to fill. NTE's system provides a real-time, neutral trading platform.

History

Founded by Gregory Rocque, NTE was conceived in 1993, launched in August 1996, and the first web-based interface was introduced in December 1997. NTE is backed by an estimated $15-20 million in funding from AT&T Ventures, Hummer Winblad Venture Partners, Crosspoint Venture Partners, Bessemer Venture Partners, and Platinum Venture Partners. The company is not yet profitable.

Vertical Market Opportunity

For years, trucking companies and shippers have been trying to co-ordinate loads with empty trucks, yet the complex web of trucking routes, and the often random needs of companies that ship products have presented problems that are difficult to solve. As a result, many trucks leave drop-off points without full loads rather than go through the hassle of trying to find shippers whose needs match their return routes. Logistics industry experts estimate that in the motor carrier industry alone, capacity may be under-utilized by as much as 50% today. This under-utilization is costing buyers and sellers of transportation services at least $31 billion annually. NTE aims to reduce some of this $15 billion a year in distribution and transaction costs from the $400 billion trucking business.

Although "freight matching" services tried to address these problems, the lack of a real-time communications medium and incompatible information technology deployment prevented the development of an effective mechanism to link shippers and carriers. NTE's executive team recognized that widespread adoption of Internet and E-commerce technologies would create a virtually seamless shipping environment that could enable supply executives to manage the logistics of information as effectively as they manage the logistics of their inventory. NTE delivers a solution to the complicated problems of the transportation business, improving supply chain performance by enabling reliable, real-time visibility for the execution of transportation transactions.

Membership Model

NTE is neutrally-owned by commercial investors and has open, qualified membership policies. NTE screens trucking companies to ensure that only the reputable and the insured are listed. To trade, members are qualified based on safety ratings, insurance, size of fleet, type of freight and credit history. NTE ensures the quality, integrity, and settlement of every transaction.

Trading Model

NTE collects shipment orders in its database, computes a market price for each one, and then matches them to truck routes provided by carriers. The database is updated instantly as new shipments are tendered, and carriers can get a list of loads which meet their route plans in seconds. NTE's system allows members to interactively match desirable rates for shipments by quoting a confirmed price for approval before it is committed by the shipper, or accepted by the carrier, in the electronic marketplace. When the delivery of the shipment is confirmed, NTE pays the carrier and invoices the shipper.

NTE creates a spot market by setting daily prices based on trading activities of several hundred fleet managers about the destinations of their vehicles and the amount of space available. It then aligns the compatible deals. NTE's pricing models use custom software to factor in the shipping route, time, date, temperature, and distance. NTE tells carriers how much profit they stand to make with each load which takes away the uncertainty that often deters truckers from taking on more cargo. NTE has defined processes, data capture and reporting, interfaces to related technologies, and even provides transportation billing and payment with third-party oversight.

Market Entry Strategy

Initially, NTE focused on the key players in a small region. After proving the business model and demonstrating the security and reliability of the trading engine, NTE began to expand its services and membership. Over the past three years, NTE has developed a robust technology infrastructure designed to meet the specific needs of the transportation industry — a system that now serves the entire country and one that would not be easily replicated.

Achieving Dominance

Currently, NTE has more than 350 members and expects to handle between 125,000 and 175,000 shipments in the next year. NTE's carrier membership includes contract carrier fleets, dedicated carrier fleets, and the private fleets of major corporations. Shipper membership includes all segments of manufacturing. NTE continues to grow its membership using a variety of both on-line and off-line marketing and sales activities. The company's challenge is to build a customer base large enough to attract even more business.

"Building a Community" — Services Added to the Trading Mechanism

NTE continues to develop new functionality with a focus on navigability, reliability, and scalability as features are added to enhance both the E-commerce system and supply chain integration. This includes Internet and Extranet tools for members. NTE's goal is to provide tight integration between the back-end systems of suppliers and buyers. In order to provide increased connectivity and integration between motor carriers and shippers, NTE established software alliances with companies such as SAP AG, Manugistics Transportation Management, McLeod Software, TMW Systems and Creative Systems. Soon, NTE will roll out software that allows companies to track day-to-day margins and costs in real time. Members who use the Extranet site can find rates, manifests, and service guides that aren't available on the Internet. NTE aims to provide members with a wide range of information to maximize their business, all accessible from one point.

Revenue Model

NTE members pay a one-time start up fee, which varies depending on how much work the company's engineers must do to mesh a member's existing databases with NTE's. Some carriers have legacy systems that require significant work, while others — without existing baggage — don't even require a service visit. NTE also collects a transaction fee based on the value of each deal. When a deal is agreed, NTE issues the contract and handles payment. As NTE accumulates data from the trading mechanism, it is likely that aggregated, sanitized information will be provided to the industry for an additional charge. Customers may also choose to pay NTE's strategic partners for integration modules that link directly to NTE.

Confidentiality and Neutrality

NTE is a neutral marketplace. Member confidentiality is preserved until a transaction is created; the identities of both parties are then revealed.

Contact Details for Further Information

National Transportation Exchange
1400 Opus Place, Suite 800
Downers Grove, IL 60515

E-mail: info@nte.net

PaperExchange

Overview

PaperExchange is an Internet marketplace for paper buyers, sellers, traders, and brokers. All grades of paper, from first quality to trim rolls, can be bought or sold on the exchange. With members in 75 countries and 24-hour site access seven days a week, the PaperExchange trading floor provides the most efficient worldwide marketplace for paper. PaperExchange is a global neutral marketplace. Members own the paper, sell the paper, buy the paper, set prices, and establish terms for transfer. All paper is bought and sold through secured, anonymous transactions. PaperExchange does not share its list of members or its transaction information.

History

Hilton Plein founded PaperExchange's predecessor company in late 1996. Initially, the company's focus was within the containerboard arena only and the real expansion of PaperExchange into all major paper grades happened after the current investors became involved in 1998. From the beginning, PaperExchange has remained focused on developing the exchange as the core of the business with additional services added to offer more value to members. The primary investors are The Kraft Group (the major investor to date), Internet Capital Group (approximately 25%), Terrapin Partners and Roger Stone (former CEO of Stone Container Corp). ICG became investor/owners in August 1999 and additional funding was received from all investors in September 1999. PaperExchange is headquartered in Boston, Massachusetts. The company is not yet profitable and is currently focused on building leadership and market share.

Vertical Market Opportunity

Extensive industry expertise is one of PaperExchange's major strengths. The founders have experience in the containerboard industry and the company has recruited industry professionals across all major paper grades. Key managers in sales, business development, marketing, and IT all come from within the pulp and paper industry and ensure that PaperExchange delivers the tools its users need.

Paper manufacturers still rely on a complex network of distributors, brokers, and reps. The result is market inefficiency and chronic imbalances between supply and demand. The founders of PaperExchange identified a large market that could benefit from an exchange system. PaperExchange more efficiently matches buyers with sellers, which is important in a volatile market with inconsistent demand. Because paper is a global business, it is subject to the many different demand cycles throughout the regional and national economies. With no current exchange-based hedging tools available, market players are exposed to influences that no one player can control. This situation is complicated by the fact that traditional pricing instruments are often late and not representative of the actual transactions taking place at any given time. PaperExchange plans to deliver a solution to these problems and may bring the paper industry its first real-time public pricing forum. If successful, PaperExchange could smooth supply and demand fluctuations and perhaps even offer risk management tools.

Membership Model

PaperExchange is owned by commercial investors and has open membership. The site is a neutral and independent site and operates autonomously from any other pulp and paper organization or company. Membership of the exchange is available to all pulp and paper industry and related industry professionals. Although only members may buy or sell on the exchange, visitors may use the service for informational purposes.

Trading Model

PaperExchange operates a true exchange with real-time pricing and on-line trade execution. The company provides a proactive matching service between buyers and sellers of paper and pulp products and related services. PaperExchange provides a bidding system that enables buyers to bid on products offered by a seller, or buyers can list requests to purchase products. PaperExchange also offers a "clearing" process and will guarantee payments by certain buyers whose creditworthiness has been approved in advance.

Market Entry Strategy

PaperExchange initially targeted sellers to gain critical mass and increase paper volume on the exchange. After gaining acceptance and participation from a large number of suppliers/manufacturers who provided product to the site, PaperExchange is now working to expand its buyer membership. PaperExchange's original product focus was on containerboard, one of the larger sectors in the pulp and paper industry. After gaining market share in this area, the company expanded to include other paper grades. Currently, the major focus is on expanding on-line offerings to include printing and writing papers. The company is also enhancing features and services available on the site.

Achieving Dominance

In October 1999, PaperExchange had over 2,000 corporate members. The Exchange is used by several hundred paper buyers and sellers in 75 countries, including nine of the top dozen suppliers in the US. To drive business in the $300 billion annual world paper market, PaperExchange relies on a variety of sales and marketing activities, including public relations, trade shows, trade and on-line advertising.

"Building a Community" — Services Added to the Trading Mechanism

The PaperExchange web site provides news, stock information, industry resource information, event calendars, equipment sales, and career and other information services. PaperExchange delivers clearing and logistics services via international partners. Credit services, back-office systems and direct links from users' systems directly to PaperExchange will be introduced shortly.

Revenue Model

PaperExchange's primary revenues are derived from a 3% transaction fee charged to suppliers for each purchase made using the service. There are no membership fees or charges for posting products for sale.

Confidentiality and Neutrality

PaperExchange is a neutral marketplace with a commitment to fairness, confidentiality, and security. PaperExchange controls access and use of the service through a combination of a customer ID, employee ID, and password. The exchange allows members to post anonymously and makes every attempt to preserve the anonymity of the parties and credit ratings until a transaction is agreed upon. When a transaction is agreed upon, both buyer and seller identities and credit ratings are revealed so that logistics and payment terms can be finalized. PaperExchange expects to be the first in the on-line paper industry to pass the stringent guidelines set for data security and privacy when it gains certification from Ernst & Young on security of data.

Contact Details for Further Information

PaperExchange
545 Boylston Street, 8th Floor
Boston, MA 02116
Phone: 1-617-536-4310

E-mail: info@paperexchange.com

PlasticsNet

www.plasticsnet.com

Overview

PlasticsNet is an electronic marketplace for the plastics industry that provides trade services to promote E-commerce and the exchange of ideas and information. Services include directories, job listings, free classified advertising, news, discussion forums, and the industry's most comprehensive database of product and service information. By aggregating thousands of products from more than 200 suppliers, PlasticsNet streamlines the purchasing process and reduces the overall cost per sale. A classic infomediary, PlasticsNet provides a "one-stop" source for the plastics industry. Products cataloged include mold components, machinery parts, software, educational materials, replacement parts and raw materials. The site allows users to search by keyword, company, and category. Diagrams, pictures, and pricing information are included.

History

In early 1994, Tim and Nick Stojka discovered a way that the Internet might be used to streamline the supply chain processes in the plastics industry and began to explore the concept for PlasticsNet. Sons of the founder of Fast Heat, a supplier to the plastics industry, the Stojka brothers grew up in the plastics business, understood industry practices and recognized the problems the Internet could solve. Chicago-based CommerX launched the PlasticsNet site in October 1995. It now houses what is said to be the first electronic commerce center for the plastics industry. Since March 1999, the site has been evolving from a trade community and sourcing guide for the plastics industry into a fully-fledged marketplace with complete E-commerce capabilities. CommerX is a private company that provides the PlasticsNet service. Second round funding was raised from the Internet Capital Group. CommerX is now in the process of raising a third round of financing.

Vertical Market Opportunity

The plastics industry is currently a $370 billion per year business, the fourth-largest manufacturing segment in the US. It is also an extremely fragmented business with more than 5,000 suppliers, more than 18,000 processors and layers of distributors and maintenance, repair and operating companies. A sound understanding of the huge, but fragmented, plastics industry presented an opportunity too good to pass by, and PlasticsNet, one of the earliest business-to-business communities, was created. From fewer than 15 employees in January 1999, PlasticsNet has already grown to 70 employees. PlasticsNet is focused on building a team that understands the traditional industry buying and selling processes and can help develop appropriate sales channels to serve plastics buyers' needs. Recruiting from traditional plastics industry leaders is a tactic used to preserve PlasticsNet's credibility and expertise.

Membership Model

PlasticsNet services are available to members free of charge. Suppliers and users must register as members before they can bid, but there are no membership or set-up fees.

Trading Model

A variety of different trading mechanisms are available depending on the type of product being purchased. PlasticsNet enables E-commerce through the on-line procurement site and the on-line marketplace and handles receivables. In PlasticsNet's exchange, auctions and reverse auctions are used primarily for excess, used, or hard-to-find products. The traditional, fixed-price model is used in the on-line catalog, a searchable database that allows customers to review products and prices from multiple manufacturers. The catalog is used for commodity-type products, and it is worth noting that the "fixed price" may be different depending on the buyer.

Market Entry Strategy

PlasticsNet was one of the first vertical B2B marketplaces and is strongly buyer-focused. In fact, all features of the site have been developed according to buyer feedback. With a focus on traffic initially, PlasticsNet targeted buyers' needs for centralized information, gradually expanding its offerings as traffic grew. It now boasts a wide array of community services, including a searchable catalog, supplier web sites, the largest on-line plastics-industry job bank, an educational database, classified postings, technical forums, and a large inventory of technical datasheets on plastics products. Because the plastics industry was not ready for E-commerce initially, the site relied on advertising revenue until 1999. Today, PlasticsNet expects the majority of revenues to come from E-commerce-related services.

Achieving Dominance

PlasticsNet currently maintains a base of 30,000 users who have registered for site-wide access. This user base is growing rapidly and already supports an average of 90,000 sessions per month. Over 165 suppliers are engaged in sales, marketing and advertising activities on PlasticsNet. PlasticsNet is in the unusual and highly desirable position of not being faced with any stiff competition. This domination of the on-line plastics market is the result of a good partnership strategy and an aggressive marketing campaign that began in 1999. Partnerships with technology partners such as Heller Financial and JD Edwards, and major trade publications that contribute content, help guarantee PlasticsNet's success. A mix of on-line (30%) and off-line (70%) marketing activities across all traditional channels (PR, events, print ads, direct marketing) also help ensure that PlasticsNet keeps ahead of the competition.

"Building a Community" — Services Added to the Trading Mechanism

Over the past four years, PlasticsNet has steadily added new services to complement and enhance the trading mechanism. An education center now offers training programs and education materials. A career center provides recruiting services, and a partnership with MatWeb offers users access to a materials database for comprehensive technical information. In addition, E-commerce features on PlasticsNet have been expanded to include on-line auctions, and users can look forward to the launch of a desktop solution for buyers. This back-office system will automate transactional sales, linking inventory and accounting systems and allow users to order from multiple suppliers on a single purchase order.

Revenue Model

PlasticsNet's revenues come from a variety of sources — transaction fees, posting fees, advertising and marketing services, and fees for back-office services and software licensing. Transaction fees vary based on product line and are expected to represent the majority of revenue by 2000. Posting fees are charged for career applications and postings. PlasticsNet collects advertising revenue and also provides an avenue for "sponsors" to survey the PlasticsNet membership on-line and charges a fee to collect this market research data. Although there is no user set-up fee for the web-based system, PlasticsNet also offers a desktop procurement solution that delivers enhanced functionality, linking partners' systems into PlasticsNet. There are set-up and consulting fees charged for the desktop procurement system software and implementation, as well as fees for back-office services such as tracking, invoicing and handling receivables.

Confidentiality and Neutrality

Registered members of PlasticsNet are uniquely identified by the system based on customer ID in order to ensure that confidentiality is maintained, as well as to automate pricing systems. Users and suppliers cannot see who is buying what, and users automatically get different prices and information based on their profile and classification.

Contact Details for Further Information

PlasticsNet.com, a service of CommerX, Inc.
350 North LaSalle Street, Suite 1000
Chicago, IL 60610
Phone: 1-312-832-9330

E-mail: trodak@plasticsnet.com

TechEx

Overview

TechEx is the leading Internet exchange for technology transfer in the life science industry. TechEx facilitates targeted communications between technology transfer offices at research institutions and corporate technology developers. The TechEx web site automatically links technology and intellectual property listings from leading research organizations to licensing executives in major life science companies. Members can scan new technology opportunities efficiently, without the distraction of inappropriate and unwanted information. Simultaneously, the network helps technology providers target interested commercial developers. TechEx is not yet profitable and recently completed first round funding.

History

Originally created by Jon Garen at the Yale University Office of Cooperative Research in 1997, a patent application for TechEx, as a way to leverage the Internet as a medium for technology transfer, was filed in 1998. Perceived to have significant commercial value by Yale University, TechEx was exclusively licensed to Intellectual Property Technology Exchange, Inc. in July 1999. Spinning TechEx out as a separate, for-profit company, not only provides the capital necessary for aggressive growth, but also positions the company to take advantage of commercial opportunities that were not the focus of a non-profit university. Sculley Brothers LLC is an investor in TechEx.

Vertical Market Opportunity

Jon Garen and Yale University recognized that the process of getting technology out of an academic institution is inefficient unless a researcher has a strong relationship with their institution's technology transfer office, and the case manager within that office has established contacts with potential buyers of the technology. Garen believed that the Internet could solve some of these relationship issues by better targeting technologies to the people who need them. The TechEx exchange was launched to serve the needs of the life science industry which represents 70% of the technology transfer market. TechEx already has a strong hold on the academic institutions that spend more than $700 million annually to license life science technology. The company is focused on developing value-added services as it seeks to gain critical mass in the almost $6 billion annual world market for technology transfer in the life science industry (including related merger and acquisition activity). Only after reaching critical mass in life sciences does TechEx plan to expand into other verticals by superimposing their model into information technology and physical sciences markets.

Membership Model

TechEx is owned by commercial investors and has open, qualified membership. Participation is restricted to technology transfer officers from accredited research institutions; corporate licensing professionals capable of bringing early stage inventions to market; and credible investors capable of providing financial assistance to commercialization efforts. TechEx is diligent about confirming institutional or corporate affiliation of members as well as authenticating that the person in the organization has the authority to buy or sell technology. Access to the TechEx service is password protected and secure; casual users are not permitted to use the system.

Trading Model

TechEx implements a post and browse trading model with automated, anonymous e-mail communication and push e-mail notification. TechEx's web site allows registered researchers to describe the technologies they want to sell, while allowing company managers to create "interest profiles" describing the kinds of research they want to track. Once a technology is posted, the system uses a keyword and semantic search function to send e-mail notifications and single-page abstracts to buyers whose profiles indicate potential interest.

By pushing technology directly to appropriate recipients, based on their own self-described interests, and returning a recipient list to universities, TechEx will replace current marketing practices with a more efficient approach. Trading and clearing functions are currently in development with a strategic partner and will be deployed once TechEx begins charging transaction fees.

Market Entry Strategy

Launched by Yale, TechEx initially targeted research institutions with a solution to facilitate academic technology transfer activities. The university platform was particularly beneficial for TechEx since not-for-profit organizations frequently have access to technology earlier than corporations, and because more and more corporations are outsourcing research to universities. In fact, the research institution holds enormous credibility in the life science vertical. This is due primarily to strong academic and medical ties that are not as prevalent in other technology transfer markets such as IT and physical science. With a strong offering for research institutions now in place and widely embraced, TechEx has a critical mass of institutional users and is more likely to be able to attract corporate participation. After the technology platform is fully developed, TechEx plans to expand into other technology transfer markets. Eventually, TechEx also hopes to broaden corporate participation to facilitate corporate-to-corporate technology transfers.

Achieving Dominance

With over 600 members, including biotechnology and pharmaceutical companies, investment firms, and research organizations, TechEx boasts an average of 25 technologies listed weekly and has 1,900 technologies currently listed in the database. To date, more than 50,000 connections have taken place between research scientists and licensing professionals. The TechEx web site now tracks about half of the 50 to 60 new life-science technologies developed weekly across the country. A strong customer service program is focused on ensuring that existing members will make the transition as TechEx begins charging membership fees for the first time. In order to grow rapidly, TechEx has outsourced all technology development and relies on strategic partnerships to drive content offerings and attract new users. Traditional marketing across both on-line and off-line media are being used to attract new members and educate existing members about new services.

"Building a Community" — Services Added to the Trading Mechanism

In conjunction with respected strategic partners, TechEx plans to provide critical informational content around its listings in order to allow buyers to more accurately and quickly make decisions about whether to pursue a technology. Some features in development include providing members with instant access to related research, information about competitive technologies, and background information on both the inventor and his institution. A preformatted search of the patent landscape also enhances the technology description and matching service. In an attempt to increase switching costs, TechEx is providing links to the information systems of strategic partners including aggregating services that target the life sciences market. This makes it difficult for corporations to use a competing exchange since their "supplier" is tied directly to TechEx.

Revenue Model

Access to TechEx is completely free to research institutions in order to encourage technology listings. An annual fee charged for corporate membership allows unlimited use of the system by the organization (rather than per user license). As TechEx develops value enhancements and is able to become instrumental to the technology transfer process, the company plans to charge a transaction fee for deals closed through the system. Anticipating demand for industry data generated by the trading system, TechEx plans to publish technology trends and charge users fees for access to this information.

Confidentiality and Neutrality

TechEx users are aware of technology sources, but not of who else is looking at the technology. The system indicates how many other companies are looking at the same technology. Member profiles are maintained in absolute confidentiality so that neither competing corporations nor researchers are privy to the specific interests of others.

Contact Details for Further Information

Intellectual Property Technology Exchange, Inc.
25 Science Park, Box 20
New Haven, CT 06511
Phone: 1-203-865-5522

E-mail: jerry.williamson@techex.com

References and
Bibliography

Chapter 1: What are B2B Exchanges?

The Heyday of Auctions, The Economist, 23–30 July 1999

B2B Revolution, by Dana Blankenhorn, IntellectualCapital.com, 3 June 1999

B2B Boom: The Web's Trillion Dollar Secret, Business 2.0, September 1999

Chapter 2: B2B is Where the Profits Will Be, On-line

Resizing On-line Business Trade, Forrester Research Inc. Report, November 1998

The Global Market Forecast for Internet Usage and Commerce: Based on Internet Commerce Market Model, (Version 5), International Data Corp., June 1999

B2B: 2B or not 2B? Goldman Sachs Investment Research on E-Commerce/Internet, 14 September 1999

B2B Boom: The Web's Trillion Dollar Secret, Business 2.0, September 1999

Your Choice, Andersen Consulting study, 1998
(see http://www.ac.com/showcase/ecommerce/ecom_efuture.html)

eEurope Takes Off, Andersen Consulting study, 1999
(see http://www.ac.com/showcase/ecommerce/ecom_efuture.html)

How Culture Clash Sank the Toys "R" Us Deal, by Bernhard Warner and Miguel Helft, Industry Standard, 30 August-6 September 1999

Get Rich...Quixtar!, by Todd Lappin, Business 2.0, August 1999

General Motors Looks to the Future with Internet Unit, by Fara Warner, Wall Street Journal, 11 August 1999

Chapter 3: Why B2B Exchanges are Developing on the Internet

Anatomy of New Market Models, Forrester Research, Inc. Report, by Varda Lief, February 1999

Chicago Board of Trade History
(see http://www.cbot.com/pointsofinterest/visitor/
about_backgrounder.html)

Chapter 4: "Its NOT About the Technology, Stupid!"

A Virtual Trading Option for the Reinsurance Arena, Insurance Networking, 1 May 1999, (available at http://info.Catex.com/
hamilton/Catex/newsArticle?articleID=18)

B2B Boom: The Web's Trillion Dollar Secret, Business 2.0, September 1999

B2B: 2B or not 2B?, Goldman Sachs Investment Research on E-Commerce/Internet, 14 September 1999

Chapter 5: Membership and Ownership Models

A Blueprint for Success, The Toronto Stock Exchange, 8 October 1998

The Right Way Forward. A Review of the Stock Exchange of Hong Kong's Monopoly Status, International Securities Consultancy Research Report, by Robert Fell CBE CB, Susan Selwyn and W William A Woods, published by ISI Publications.

Chapter 6: Trading Models

Goldman Sachs Investment Research on Internet Technology, 9 November 1998

Chapter 7: Strategic Partnership Models

Bloomberg by Bloomberg, Michael Bloomberg, published by Wiley

Chapter 8: Revenue Models

Catex Reinsurance Reports 100th Deal, electronic transaction system broadens types of postings, Journal of Commerce, 17 February 1999 (see http://info.Catex.com/hamilton/Catex/newsArticle?articleID=17)

Chapter 10: Play to Win — the Need to Dominate

Let's Get Vertical, by Mahanbir Sawhney and Steven Kaplan, Business 2.0, September 1999

A Virtual Trading Option for the Reinsurance Arena, Insurance Networking, 1 May 1999 (see http://info.Catex.com/hamilton/Catex/newsArticle?articleID=18)

Chapter 11: Maintain Commercial Neutrality

On-line. Offshore, the corporate brochure of the Bermuda Stock Exchange (www.bsx.com)

Catex Press Release: *Catex Obtains Capital and Commitments for Future Trading*
(see http://info.Catex.com/hamilton/Catex/press?articleID=11)

For Arthur Andersen's independent report on MetalSite's business practices
(see http://metalsite.net/Welcome_to_MetalSite.cfm?target=admin/businessprinciples.cfm&ads=ad_bizprince.cfm))

Euromoney, September 1999 (see the "BrokerTec" story)

The Financial Times, Derivatives Supplement, 20 September 1999

Chapter 12: Ensure Transparency and Integrity

IOSCO Core Principles for Securities Market Regulations

B2B Revolution, by Dana Blankenhorn, IntellectualCapital.com, 3 June 1999

Chapter 16: 2B or not 2B On-line?

dyb.com, The Economist, 18 September 1999

Competing in the Digital Age: How the Internet will Transform Business, Booz Allen & Hamilton and the Economist Intelligence Unit (summary available at www.bah.com), May 1999

Tech Tattle, a column by Ahmed Elamin, The Royal Gazette, Bermuda, October 1999

Bibliography

Bloomberg by Bloomberg
Michael Bloomberg, published by Wiley

The Death of Distance
Frances Cairncross, published by Orion Business Books

Business @ The Speed of Thought: Using a Digital Nervous System
Bill Gates, published by Warner Books

Net Gain: Expanding Markets through Virtual Communities
John Hagel III and Arthur G Armstrong, published by Harvard
Business School Press

Net Worth: Shaping Markets when Customers Make the Rules
John Hagel III and Marc Singer, published by Harvard Business
School Press

*New Rules for the New Economy: 10 Radical Strategies for a
Connected World*
Kevin Kelly, published by Viking

Cybercorp: The New Business Revolution
Dr. James Martin, published by Amacom

Alien Intelligence: Winner Takes Most
Dr. James Martin, awaiting publication

Inside the Tornado
Geoffrey A Moore, published by HarperBusiness

Crossing the Chasm
Geoffrey A Moore, published by HarperBusiness

Opening Digital Markets: Battle Plans and Business Strategies for Internet Commerce
Walid Mougayar, published by McGraw Hill

Journals and magazines:

- Business 2.0
- Business Week
- Forbes
- Industry Standard
- Inter@ctive Week
- Red Herring
- The Economist
- WIRED